JOURNEY OF FAITH

Anthony Anei Majok

Edited by Jenan Jones Benson
With
Barbara Baillet Moran
And
The Writers' Group of the Triad

Order this book online at www.trafford.com
or email orders@trafford.com

Most Trafford titles are also available at major online book retailers.

© Copyright 2011 Anthony Anei Majok.

All rights reserved. No part of this publication may be reproduced, stored in a retrieval system, or transmitted, in any form or by any means, electronic, mechanical, photocopying, recording, or otherwise, without the written prior permission of the author.

Printed in the United States of America.

ISBN: 978-1-4269-8177-7 (sc)
ISBN: 978-1-4269-8178-4 (hc)
ISBN: 978-1-4269-8179-1 (e)

Library of Congress Control Number: 2011912836

Trafford rev. 08/12/2011

Trafford PUBLISHING www.trafford.com

North America & international
toll-free: 1 888 232 4444 (USA & Canada)
phone: 250 383 6864 ♦ fax: 812 355 4082

Forward

While serving on the board of the Writers' Group of the Triad in Greensboro, NC, I've received many phone calls requesting the organization's assistance. Only one is written in my heart and mind forever.

Anthony Majok's search for an editor ended when he recounted for me his 17-year journey from war-ravaged Sudan to the United States. There was no doubt that I would be a small part of sharing his story.

For the next two years, I helped craft the amazingly inspiring story upon which you are embarking. The experience unfolded more richly as the project progressed. Early efforts, with indispensible assistance from Writers' Group of the Triad members Barbara Baillet Moran, June Wilson Read, Sandra Redding, Anya Russian, Melanie Arrowwood Wilcox and friends Blake Fisher, Sam Moffitt and Patricia Russian focused on Anthony's request that we "Americanize" his admirable writing. Learning and writing in English as a second language is not a task for the timid.

As the language became clearer, the story revealed itself to be much more than a tale of suffering, loss, disease and extreme poverty. The theme resounding from beginning to end is one of gargantuan faith in God—that unique trust that brings praise to God while bombs fall, a confident hope that doesn't waver as one looks death in the eye, and an unfaltering assurance that the Almighty is all-sufficient.

Author and editor extraordinaire Barbara Baillet Moran deserves an extra word of appreciation. Without her invaluable input into the final editing process, this story would be far less readable.

Lastly, thank you Anthony for sharing your story and your faith with the goal of education while also generating funds to construct schools in the country of South Sudan, born on July 9, 2011.

--Jenan Jones Benson

Note to the Reader

I have made every effort to convey the truth of my journey, but some events have been compressed to better meet the needs of the story. As with all memoirs, dialogue represents the essence of conversations long past, rather than direct quotes.

You may wonder why I've recounted my horrible story of surviving war from the age of seven. I hope to help readers understand the causes of Sudanese civil war and the suffering heaped upon the people of Southern Sudan, Southern Kordofan, Blue Nile and Abyei. Allow my experience to help you reflect upon your own life and strengthen you to overcome your own challenges. I pray that you will gain faith and confidence in God in times of both suffering and abundance and trust that He will see you through every hardship as you travel life's journey.

Prologue

One morning I was sitting on the riverbank when I heard an airplane. Before I could figure out where the sound was coming from, the plane started to release many thousands of tons of bombs. Surprisingly, none of those bombs exploded because the land was all covered by water and mud. So the bombs that had landed on the water and on mud had sunk into the mud and did not explode. By the grace of God, those falling on dry land didn't explode either. No one could understand this, but I suggested that maybe God was really tired of helpless and innocent children being killed every day for years on end. God perhaps had decided not to let any one of us get killed the first day the warplane Antonov bombed us.

Dedication

This book is dedicated to my Mother Akon Wol, My father Majok Acien, my friend Cornelius Achuil, Boys/Girls of Sudan, to those who had lost their lives during Sudan civil war and to all those who had suffered during their long journey to freedom.

Chapter One:
A Boy of Majok Akot Tong

As a small boy in the early 1980s, my days were filled with family and a beautiful countryside. All day my brothers, sisters, and I would play by a stream and hop in for a swim when it was hot. We played hide and seek in the nearby forest, climbed trees and swung from their branches. We'd snack on wild fruits. Then we'd gather mud by the bank of the stream and create cows, goats, donkeys, camel, and sheep; you might call that the Play-doh of Africa. You see, my early days were spent in the village of Majok Akot Tong, so named for a man called Akot Tong, in southern Sudan. Yes, the same place that was fighting for its independence well into the 21st century. My motherland is located south of Egypt, to the west of Ethiopia and the east of the Red Sea. The Nile River runs through the country; Arabic nations are relatively near.

Those Middle Eastern neighbors had a strong influence. In addition to our Dinka dialogue, Arabic was also spoken in my village. Although my father was a Christian and practicing Catholic, he had three wives. Thus, our home was actually a big compound with four houses, all built with grass on top and mud on the bottom. My father, Majok Acien, lived in the center home and each wife and her children had a dwelling. Between my mother, Akon Wol, the second wife and the other wives, our family had thirteen children.

We were farmers and ranchers, providing for our own needs with abundant crops such as sorghum, millets, ground nuts, sesame, corn, okra and pumpkin. More than 160 head of cattle, 200 goats and more than 60 sheep grazed our pastures and provided both milk and meat. Each day would end with my parents telling stories to help teach us life's lessons. It was a peaceful and beautiful childhood. But long before I reached adulthood, those happy days would fade away as quickly as a sweet dream.

Chapter Two: A Visit with Grandmother

I fled my motherland Sudan in 1987, at the tender age of seven as a result of civil war in the region. Sudan is one of many countries around the world that has been at war for most of its history. After the country declared independence from the British and Egyptian occupation in January 1, 1956; Sudan did not enjoy its freedom. War immediately broke out between the new government, controlled by Arabs, in the north and the rebels from the south and the marginalized areas of the indigenous people of Sudan. Political, economic, racial, and religious conflicts as well as slavery were the factors that contributed to war.

Conflict lasted from 1956 until 1972 when the war was brought to an end by the peace accord shared by the World Council and the Africa Conference of Churches in Addis Ababa [the capital city of Ethiopia], and signed by the people of the south and marginalized areas and the central government of Sudan. According to the agreement, southerners were given some freedom in the country in order to quiet them down and the southerners agreed even though they had not achieved all their demands. During the 16 years of war, tens of thousands of southerners were killed or displaced from their homes.

Despite the peace deal, there was constant violation of the peace by the government. In 1983, the President of Sudan, Ja'afar Nimeiry, declared that he wanted to transform Sudan into a Muslim Arab state. He also went too far by dividing the south into three regions and instituting sharia law. All the indigenous people of Sudan were increasingly suffering from northern domination and injustices. In addition to that, they were running out of patience and became angry at the policy of dividing the indigenous people of Sudan in order to kill one another. These factors led to another war breaking out between the Sudan People Liberation Army (SPLA) that was led by Dr. Garang de Mabior and the Sudan central government under the president Nimeiry in 1983. This continued for about three years until Sadiq al Mahdi overthrew Nimeiry toward the end of 1985. Al Mahdi took over while Nimeiry was visiting the United States. Al Mahdi was sworn in as the prime minister of Sudan and during his first year in the office in 1986, the Khartoum government under his command recruited militia forces to destabilize the civilian population in the region of south Sudan. The militia forces that were recruited by Al Mahdi were sent to southern Sudan to destroy everything in the villages. The militias did not reach our village until 1987.

During that seventh summer of my life, Grandmother Arek Manyuel paid a weeklong visit to our home village. The night before her departure, she asked my mother if I could go lived with her for some time in her village, which was 10 hours away. My mother asked me if I was interested in going. I did like the idea and I was very excited and anxiously waiting for the darkness to pass so my grandmother and I could start our journey early in the morning. I was filled with happiness because Grandmother had been very kind to me while visiting our home.

We went to bed and when Grandmother heard the cock crowing, she woke me up. We walked non-stop for hours, something I had never done before, and reached our destination very hungry and tired around 4:00 p.m. After a 30-minute rest, we fixed more food than we could eat. Grandmother and I talked until bedtime.

Grandmother's village was called Panraang, which means a village with some trees, and was west of my village. The two thousand and five hundred residents were farmers, fisher people and hunters.

Once in bed, she told me a story about how God created heaven and earth with everything on earth including human beings, followed by stories regarding our traditional way of life. I have discovered during my life journey around the world that Grandmother's stories are meaningful and important to me. I still remember three of those stories.

Her first story, about carelessness and its consequences, is still in the back of my mind. She told me that, once upon a time, there were no tall mountains, buildings, trees or any other kind of tall thing in nature. This was because heaven was too close to the earth according to Dinka traditional beliefs. She said that there are many bridges to heaven where people could visit and find God. There was no too much suffering and life was enjoyable on earth. People could live thousands of years before they died. There was plenty of food. People could gather grains of maize or corn from their farms dry them and then put in the Dinka local mill called Dong.

A Dong is usually made from a wood which is about fifty to hundred inches thick and is about three to four feet tall. Dong looks like a mortar. The person creating it makes a hole in a piece of wood and smoothy it inside and out. A four to five foot stick called lek serves as a pestle for crushing the grain. People would place one grain of maize inside a Dong and put the leek on the top of it. It was left there for a while to grind it without anyone pushing the lek because it was believe that a person who could pound grain could hit the sky and God might get angry at such an act.

Grandmother said that all human beings had been living that way for many centuries with a good relationship with God until one day when careless, impatient women decided that she would go ahead and start pounding the grain herself because it was taking a long time for the grain to crush itself. As she was pounding the grain, she raised the pestle so high that she hit the sky. Heaven started moving far away from people. Now, there were no means of traveling to God and life become harder and harder. She cautioned me to listen to people's advice always, wherever I maybe. She also advised me to respect the law all the time and to avoid handling things carelessly, for those who are careless usually harm themselves or could even take their own lives without clear knowledge of what they are doing.

This tale gives me the idea that my grandmother was predicting the situation I was going to face later on in my life. I believed that sharing this story was her way of preparing me for future challenges.

Another story Grandmother Arek related to me was about seeing a duck trying to swallow a very big frog as she walked on her farm by a river. She stepped closer to watch the fight. The duck had swallowed the entire frog except the front legs and the head. The duck tried really hard to swallow the frog but the frog keeps spreading its front legs wider. At long last, the duck realized that the frog was not able to give in to death, and released the frog from its mouth. The injured frog then jumped back into the water, singing the song of struggle and victory. Grandmother told me that she had learned from the frog that life is made up of struggle and challenges. She told me to be ready to meet any test and I should not give up easily. No matter what happened, I have to struggle hard to save my life.

My grandmother's last story told of a woman who gave birth to only one son and she was concerned about his future. She kept him with her at all times until he was ten years old. One day, he asked if she would allow him to go and play with neighboring children, and she approved her son's request. She was concerned that her son might make friends with bad children, spoiling his future.

He began playing with the local children every day and soon brought home his good friend, a boy his own age. The woman invited the friend for lunch the next day. She prepared three boiled eggs; her son's friend ate two eggs and her son had only one egg. When the mother learned this, she asked her son to drop that friend and find another one. She went on testing her son's friends until one of the boys ate one egg, her son had one egg and then the friend insisted that they needed to share the third egg.

Her son was very excited that he had found such a friend and couldn't wait to tell his mother. She advised him to be friends with that boy forever. She said that such a friend would be loyal, that he would never abandon him. Many years later, their village came under a severe famine and the two were still friends and helped one another like brothers, enabling both to survive.

I was excited to live with Grandmother who was very resourceful and could tell me new things about life. I was also happy to be in that village because I had met new children who became my friends. I thought that my happiness would last forever; actually, it did not last much longer.

One evening before I had spent a full week with Grandmother, the village came under attack from Arab militias called murahaleen who were backed up by the current regime. They start shooting at everybody in the village. Many lay dead or unconscious, and I was confused as to what I should do. I tried to run into the bush but I kept falling down.

Then when Grandmother noticed that I was overcome by fear, and that I could not run by myself, she came back to me and grasped my arms, and put me on her back. She started running with me as one of the attackers on horseback was chasing and shooting at us. But Grandmother was around sixty years old and could not run fast with me on her back. She kept running despite the shooting until we reached the bushes where we were lucky to find a hole within a huge bush. She threw herself into the hole with me on her back. She closed my mouth with her hands so that I could not cry out or breathe loudly because the attacker was still very near to us and could hear us. The attacker fired more than fifty fire shots into the bush before returning to the village where the shooting intensified for more than an hour and a half.

They captured more than five hundred people, tied their hands and put about four hundred of them in a large building in size of a church known as lauk in Dinka, where animals such as goats, sheep and cattle are normally kept at night. Then they closed the door really tight and set the building on fire. Many of them were children, women, elderly and disabled people who were unable to run to the bush to save their lives.

Grandmother and I could hear them crying out for help; unfortunately, no one came to their rescue and they were left to die cruelly in the fire. Up to today, I still recall one of the victims calling for God's mercy and his forgiveness to be upon their souls and that God may take their spirits to heaven. Of course, those memories always haunt me and make me numb every time I think about them. I also recognized the voices of the children that I used to play with crying for help inside the giant flame of fire and tornado of thick smoke. But Grandmother and I were helpless to rescue them from that painful, brutal, and inhumane death. Their cries lasted for about three minutes and then the people started to burst aloud like bombs.

Some minutes later, the murahaleen began to complain of the dreadful smell. After destroying the village and everything in it, the attackers then tortured their prisoners. All women and teenage girls were raped and circumcised just for fun since they knew that female circumcision is not practiced in Dinka culture; men were castrated. Some ears, hands, arms and legs were amputated. The murahaleen set the remaining structures on fire and left.

When we came back to the village, we found many dead bodies all over the place. I was shocked and fainted because I had never seen a dead person before. Grandmother then laid me on the traditionally made bed composed of a wooden frame and a mattress made of rope and animal skins where I rested for about three hours until I regained my consciousness.

The population was reduced by fifty percent. Those who had survived started returning home one by one. As their number grew to about fifteen people, they started digging graves for burial the same day, according to Dinka tradition. But their problems were just beginning, as there was no medical care for the wounded. The injured villagers began to die. The survivors gathered in a large home where they could spend their night together as a group. When night came, the village was as silent as if it had been a ghost town for a hundred years. No one slept that night. Even I did not sleep, having nightmares as if the attackers were attacking us again. I kept whispering to my grandmother, "They are coming, let us run away, let us run away. "

After a miserable night, I asked to return to my parents' village. I thought that the attack was meant for Grandmother's village alone, and the militias could come back anytime and shoot us again. She told me to wait for the funeral and then she would be able to take me back. I did not like the idea of spending more time there but I had no choice. Grandmother told me that it was our traditional belief for me to attend the funeral service if someone died while I was in the village. I did not know my way back to our village, so I couldn't have left my grandmother and gone home by myself.

So I spent a few more days at Grandmother's village waiting for the funeral. The atmosphere in the village was very sad. No one felt like talking. There were no children to play with me, and I was even not in a mood to play because many of the children that I used to play with were shot dead during the attack. Many of the children were missing. In addition to that, the village was like a ghost village, and it was frightening to live there.

After we attended the funeral, Grandmother and I set out on our journey back to our village. We traveled once again for about ten hours non-stop. When we arrived at our village, we found that my parents had received the news about the shooting, and they had been worried about my grandmother and me. I felt safer and slept well that night.

Chapter Three:
A Line of Monsters

I spent one month with my parents thinking that such a horrible incident would never happen to me again; I was not to be that fortunate. Without the knowledge of villagers in southern Sudan, the Khartoum government had trained, armed, and mobilized all the Arab tribes against them. They were told to go to southern Sudan and the marginalized areas and kill everybody there. The government also told the militia to take whatever they liked in Southern Sudan, including children, cows and women. Two months after the first shooting, the government of Sudan and militias launched a major attack against all the villages in the southern region of Sudan.

One night when we were sleeping in our village and all the young villagers were dancing the summer traditional cultural dance called Loor Agar, our village was attacked. The murahaleen started to shoot people who were dancing a mere ten minutes away from our home. The shooting awaked us all and we rushed out of the house. As my father was trying to open the door, he was shot in the chest and felt down on the ground, unable to move. We managed to open the door and started to run separately in different directions, leaving my suffering father lying on the floor as we ran for our lives.

I ran as fast as I could until I reached the bush where I hid for a couple of hours. Then I started to walk into the heart of the forest by myself. I didn't know where my mother and my three and five-year-old sisters were. Both my brothers had been at the dance and weren't hurt during the shooting. They too had managed to run on their own into the forest along with other villagers. That night, everything in all of southern Sudan was destroyed. The villages were burned down into ashes, all cattle were taken, and many people including children were abducted and were taken as slaves. The water was polluted, and many people lost some part of their bodies. Some suffered sexual mutilation. The surrounding area resembled the California wild fires.

While I was wandering in the forest alone, I had several attacks from hyena. I avoided them by climbing trees at dark for three nights. The Arab attackers were still following us and warplanes were also bombing the forest and the entire region throughout each day. The forest was ablaze, killing many living things hiding there. Although merely a boy of seven, I managed to survive all those threats for three days.

Suddenly, a miracle happened. As I was resting on a tree, I then saw my brothers, Garang (Noon) who was fourteen and Santino Acien who was nine! I burst into tears calling their names. My voice scared those walking with them, but my brothers knew my voice very well and started running toward me. We met in the middle and hugged one another. The other villagers rejoined us and asked about my parents. I told them that my father was shot and that I was not so sure about the condition of other family members.

After a few minutes' rest, an older man named Deng Deng urged us to restart the journey. I asked my brothers whether we were going back to our village, but Deng Deng said it wasn't safe to return. We followed him east where there was no fighting. Tall, thick grass and thick trees with sharp thorns that could cut your skin like a knife made it difficult for us to walk fast, as attackers continued to track us.

Darkness was another obstacle we encountered. When we traveled at night, it was difficult for us to see what was on the ground, how best to move along, and whether we were under attack from both Arab militias and wild animals. There was an incident where five people were attacked and eaten by hyenas and lions. So, Deng Deng decided that we needed to hold on to each other's clothes, travel in one line and stay close together. We should sit down in a line in case of an animal attack. He insisted that this tactic would save some lives. We then traveled for several days and nights implementing his advice but that did not prevent deaths. All in all, many people lost their lives from airstrikes, ground shooting and animal attacks.

Two weeks later, we arrived at the bank of Wau River where we met about three hundred and fifty people who were also running away from the civil war. Many were boys ranging in age from six to ten. A famous chief in the Dinka tribe, Ayiin Madut, led them. They were lucky to have many adults who could help chief Ayiin with the small children and various problems. We joined this group and began to walk together, taking a long journey toward Ethiopia.

By that time, we were able to escape from ground attacks, but there were still many obstacles ahead of us. One of the problems was Wau River had flooded, making it hard to cross. There was one hand-made boat that could carry four people including the driver, but there were about six hundred people to transport. The leaders decided that those who knew how to swim could swim, while small children and non-swimmers would go by boat. One group after another jumped into the river. The strong current carried many away, as they were weakened by the sixteen day journey without good food. Crocodiles and hippopotamuses ate others.

In the middle of this nightmare, we were able to laugh at some funny things that happened to those who were victims of the river. A man called Dhalil, who happened to be toothless, would sink into the water for some seconds and then stick his head up, crying for help. But his cry made everyone laugh including those who rescued him because his gum was funny to see. After a minute, an older Good Samaritan named Dut Garang ran over and rescued Dhalil. He was almost half dead and could not breathe for about five minutes until another elder, Daniel Maroor, put his mouth on Dhalil's nose and started to suck out the water. He began to sneeze, then vomit and finally took breath. Everyone who was laughing, including me, was ashamed of our laughter at him and we felt sorry for that. He was given a place to rest by the river while those on the other side of the river were advised to take extra caution while swimming. After he had rested for a while, he was put on the boat with three children and successfully reached the other side of the river; that was a great relief.

When my turn came, two of my cousins and I were put on the boat and started to sail across the river; When we were about to reach the shore, the boat was overpowered and overturned by the current. One of my cousins called Anei Anei was hit on the neck by the boat pedal; he drowned and died on the spot. The driver, my other cousin and I were rescued, but not before we came close to drowning as well, our lungs filled with water. I was lying down vomiting and unconscious for an hour. When my cousin, Akol, and I were revived and finally crossed, we then started walking again.

I approached Deng Deng with my older brothers Garang and Acien and told them that I would not travel any more if there were more wild animals and rivers. But my brothers and Deng Deng did not allow me to lose hope. They had encouraged me to keep traveling with him and promised me that he would protect us. He assured me that rivers and animals yet to come would be no more dangerous and that we'd already survived a lot traveling these many days. I was then convinced and then agreed to go with him even if I was still doubtful and feeling terrible pain.

After traveling for about two to three hours, the condition of my feet and legs grew worst. I was not able to walk faster nor was I able to travel more than thirty minutes at a time, making it difficult for Deng Deng and my brothers to keep up with the rest of the group. However, Garang, Acien and Deng Deng did not abandon me. They keep encouraging me to never give up and keep moving even if I was overwhelmed by severe pain. Their words of advice inspired me and I was able to gain some confidence to walk a little bit faster again. But given all my efforts, the four of us still stayed about twenty minutes behind the group, as I had to have frequent two to three minute breaks. I was scared to death because we had several attacks from wolves and hyenas during that time.

When we'd lagged behind for about an hour, both children and older people began having trouble walking, too. Since the number of the disabled kept increasing and many people were singled out by wild animals and even being killed, Chief Ayiidit and Deng Deng suggested that the whole group needed to slow down their speed, and walk close to each other. Strong adults were asked to carry suffering children. Deng Deng promised me that he would carry me when I needed help. That promise gave me renewed strength to travel more miles. Since we had walked for more than seven hours, Chief Ayiidit ordered the group to rest about forty five minutes. Slowly, people began to arrive at the meeting place, stretching a forty five-minute rest to over two and a half hours. Deng Deng, my brothers, and I were the last group to arrive at the resting area.

Chief asked everyone to keep quiet while he consulted with the elders to decide whether to sleep here until sunrise or to continue traveling in the dark. Everyone suggested we should sleep there. Chief told the elders to start pushing down the grass around us so we could lie down and see in case some wild animal wanted to attack us. After they had pushed the grasses down, Chief told the elders to make a big circle, and put all the children in the middle of that circle for safety purposes. Finally, he asked about ten adults to take turns watching over those who were sleeping. We slept well that night without losing any lives, though we had several hyena attacks. Those ten men chased the hyenas away by beating pieces of wood together to produce loud sounds that scared the hyenas and also alerted to us that there was an attack coming and we should prepare to defend ourselves.

When we awoke the following morning, my body felt great. I hadn't slept like that since our village was destroyed. Everyone felt the same. The trees around us were full of fruit, which we climbed to pick for breakfast. After we were full, we took some fruit with us and set off again. We walked for more than three hours until we arrived at village of Lietnhom, where we found a man hiding outside his house. We asked him why he was hiding and he told us the village had been bombed daily for the last twenty days. Before Chief Ayiidit could finish talking to the man, we heard a plane in the air and bombs began to fall on the village. We all ran back in the forest to hide. When the bombing was over, we gathered and discovered that some of us were killed during that plane attack.

Due to that loss of life, we changed our game plan, such as it was. To be safe, we decided to travel at night and rest during the day until the attacks stopped. Traveling at night also allowed us to walk closely together and to assist when the animals attacked us. The cooler night weather helped us walk long distances without suffering dehydration. After about six days, the bombings slowed and we went back to our normal schedule: travel both night and day and rest for less than five hours. The six-day break from day travel allowed our feet to heal a little and Deng Deng made me a pair of shoes from tree leaves, which allowed me to walk for a long distance without too much concern about my swollen feet.

Our journey continued as usual for about seven to eight days until we arrived at Thiet, a town that exist in Tonj region, one of the oldest and largest towns in Bahr el Ghazal region, and a very large and dangerous forest in southern Sudan known as Roor Chuol Akol [meaning the dark forest]. It has very large trees with branches extending into the path. The villagers of Thiet advised us to gather some food and some drinking water for the trip because it would take us three to four days to cross that forest and reach an area where we could find more. They also warned us about the dangerous animals in the forest, particularly the lions, hyenas, tigers and elephants.

The villagers also, warned us about the mugging birds in that forest. One of them explained to us that there were some birds that knew how to call people's names. "So don't follow that sound in case you get lost and you hear someone calling out your name," he said. One of the villagers gave us a good example on how clever those birds were. He said that one day when he and five friends were traveling across the dark forest to visit his uncle, the bird called one of his friends by name. They thought someone who knew his friend was hiding in the forest and they stopped walking in order to make sure. While they waited in silence, the bird flew near the tree, and repeated his friend's name again. They were astonished and terrified because that was their first time to hear a bird calling a person's name. Some other birds joined the bird and the birds started to dance delightfully and sing a very sweet song, with voices like a church choir. Although he and his friends were afraid, they stood there to watch and listen.

While they were watching and listening to birds, they heard a noise from behind, and instantly they were attacked by a group of lions. The villagers battled with two big lions for almost two hours until they were able to chase the lions away, with one villager losing an eye and breaking an arm. The lions had distanced themselves away from the villagers, but were not out of sight. When the villagers tried to leave, the lions followed them.

When night came, the villagers decided to climb the big trees and spent the whole night together in one big tree. The lions spent their night under that tree. When morning came, the villagers saw the group of lions lying under the tree waiting for them. The villagers started to break some branches from the tree and threw them at the lions, chasing the lions away.

The villagers then carefully jumped down from the tree one by one. When the villagers resumed their journey, they again heard the choir of birds and the lions returned to attack. This continued for three days until the villagers made it through Roor Chuol Akol.

The villagers compared the birds to brokers in the market place, luring the buyer to the seller. The birds got the prey's attention by calling their names, and then sent a message to the lions. If the lions managed to kill that prey, the birds would share with the lions or take the leftover food. So the villagers advised us to be careful and organized in order to cross Roor Chuol Akol.

The chief of that village came to chief Ayiindit and gave him some spears for protection in case the wild animals attacked us while we were crossing the dark forest. The spears were the very weapons which the five villagers used to defend themselves. The villagers also gave about fifteen to twenty calabashes for carrying water, which was kind, but not enough to hold three to four days of water for our group that now numbered about two thousand. Lastly, the chief of that village told us we were very unlucky to have come to his village, because the food storage areas had been bombed and destroyed.

Hearing that sad news, I was devastated and hopeless. Tears started to drop from my eyes. Other children who were traveling with us cried too. Even the big people were weakened by the journey, and were not able to resist hunger any more. I was depressed because I had been traveling more than twenty five days depending on wild fruits I found in the forest. I was tired of eating wild fruits every day. I was hoping to eat hot, real food before we left that village. The villagers were generous to us and I felt that they could provide us with some food after we rested. We children who were crying were consoled by older people, and promised that, with many villages ahead of us we could find real food and every one of us would eat until we were satisfied.

After that, Chief Ayii praised the chief and villagers for the support and solidarity they had shown to us. Chief Ayiin Madut also added that God the creator would pour his blessing upon that village and be with them always in happiness and sorrows. The villagers gave us their wishes that we would overcome any obstacle in our way and that we would all reach our destination safely.

Night was approaching, so we decided to spend the night at the border of Roor Chuol Akol and then start the journey. It was advisable for anyone who needed to cross the dark forest to begin traveling early in the day in order to learn about the dark forest during the daytime and be ready for the night.

We then started our preparation for that morning's journey. Some people were sent to swim and fetch water at a nearby pool. Other adults were to go to the forest and gather some wild fruits. They brought some water and fruits, and we all ate that small meal. When it was time to sleep, children were together in a circle as usual, with some watching over those who were sleeping.

I was not able to sleep that night because I was so afraid to die. In addition to that, I was having a vision of a dark forest that I kept drawing in my head which contained a list of monsters I saw coming toward me while I was awake that night. I woke up Garang by whispering in his ears and told him that there were many monsters attacking us. My brother was also afraid and he went and woke up Deng Deng who was sleeping next to us. Deng Deng got up and looked carefully around to see what we were talking about but he could not see anything. He then realized it was the fear or imagination about the monster that was in my mind. He told me to lie down and close my eyes for sleep but when I did, I saw in a vision the lion standing over me, trying to eat me. I stood up and started running and crying, waking up everyone and many people joined me in crying. I was then caught, calmed down and advised that nothing would kill me. But I did not believe them so I stayed awake for the whole night with Deng and Garang guarding me until morning.

Chapter Four:

The next morning, the chief awakened those who were still asleep and we then journeyed toward Roor Chuol Akol in a close, single line. We walked for about four miles from the village very quietly without talking to one another. I was having too much inner talk in my mind trying to figure out how dangerous the forest would be and how could I survives in such a world. Finally some part of my mind told me not to worry too much because I had been in several bad conditions since our village came under attack and yet I survived. So I would be able to survive at Roor Chuol Akol. Finally, I changed my attention from negative thinking to positive as I was walking into the largest and scariest forest.

As I stepped into the forest, I immediately realized and understood why Roor Chuol Akol was a fearful forest in that part of southern Sudan. There were indeed many huge, tall trees by the roadside where one could not see anything through the tall grasses, and the surroundings were very quiet except the branches which I could see and hear dancing and whispering when some air passed by. The forest also was humid and hot which had made most of us get thirsty more quickly, for we traveled many hours without drinking. We started to drink the little water we had. We tried to drink water economically, but finished it before noon, and we were left with more than two days to cross the forest, with no water.

We traveled successfully for almost ten hours without any attack from wild animals or calling from those strange birds, and suddenly, my legs refused to move, and I started to feel as if my hair was growing real fast and big. I told Garang what was going on with me, but he told me that I was having such feelings because of the fear. He said I needed to shut up and keep moving because it was really risky to talk or take a break. I was left with no choice but to keep quiet and continue walking; otherwise, no one would wait for me. My legs kept getting worse and worse as we were walking at a very fast speed.

In no time, I heard the cat "Dut-dit, Dut-dit," and many birds joined in to sing. The birds were singing a very nice melody but none of us paid attention to their singing. Though we ignored them, the birds were flying around us and were still singing as one guy picked a stone off the ground, and threw it at the birds, but they would not leave us alone. We listened to the birds' entertainment for a while. Later, a group of lions attacked us so we set down close to one another and started to defend ourselves. We managed to chase them away during that first attack without any fatality on our side. It was still day time and we could see the lions. We used the spears that the villagers gave us on the lions; most of them were injured.

After we had won the first battle, we went back to walking and traveled for about one hour. But the lions attacked us again. This round, the lions managed to kill some of us and ran away with them. It was night, which made it harder for us to see properly. The fight went on for some time and then, we were not able to resist them any longer. Everyone climbed up the trees where we spent the rest of the night.

When we saw it was day time, we all jumped down from the trees and started to travel again despite the fact that we were still facing threats from wild animals as well as many other obstacles. The first obstacle was that we all were thirsty. We were out of water and there was nowhere to find water. Secondly, we had no food to eat and we were afraid to go far away from the road to gather wild fruits to eat. So, we collected the morning dew on the grasses by breaking off a leaf from a tree's branch, then folded it in order to serve as a container, collected the dew into that leaf and drank whatever few drops one might have collected. That helped us a little bit and we were able to soften our throats enough to walk for another day.

We walked across the forest non-stop for the second day. When night approached, we could again hear lions roaring and hyenas clamping their mouths. Chief then told everyone to stop walking and to climb up tall trees. Climbing the trees before dark worked. That night, wild animals ate none of us because we were hiding where the animals could not reach us. We spent that night safely, but in the morning during the third day of our journey across Roor Chuol Akol, we were not able to travel because of hunger and thirst.

One of the elders, Lino Rau, decided to risk his life by walking some yards away from the roadside. He found a small type of tree called abuuk whose roots are like sweet potatoes and full of water. Abuuk roots can be useful as water and can be eaten as food. He came back to us with some of the roots of those trees in his hands and told us that there were plenty of them. We all ran there and start digging the roots. Soon, all of us were full and no longer thirsty. We were regaining some energy to walk again. We carried more roots with us that we ate as we were traveling that last day across Roor Chuol Akol. We were not able to cross the forest on the third day of our journey because the lion attacks reduced our travel time.

Finally, we arrived at the small town in Gok Arol called Chuei Bet where villagers welcomed us with water. The villagers of Chuei Bet advised us not to drink a lot of water immediately because drinking too much water might kill us since we had spent four days without any. We listened to them, drank some water, poured some into our ears, and then washed ourselves down. We rested for a while before leaving again for another village. We were lucky this time; the villagers gave us some ground nuts and peanuts.

The people of Chuei Bet were fortunate that some of their farms were not destroyed by the air bombardment against the people of southern Sudan by the Khartoum regime. The villagers were able to advise us about the path we were to travel on. They cautioned us about the wild animals we were already familiar with. The villagers said that wild animals are common starting from Roor Chuol Akol all the way to Agar and Yorol States that border Gok Arol State. The reason why there are many dangerous wild animals is because there are numerous other animals that lions and other predators depend on for food in that region.

Another thing the villagers told us was that there was a river call Bar-el-Gal, which we would reach after two days if we could walk two days continuously without much rest. We thanked the villagers for their support and advice they provided to us, and we resumed our journey again toward river Bar-el-Gal.

Traveling toward Bar-el-Gal for a one full day and half without sleeping, I started to sleep while I was walking. That made it difficult for me to keep up with the line and follow the person who was ahead of me. Many other children were having the same problem, so we were a band of sleepwalking child. I would leave the road and wander into the forest but the caring and observant, Acien would pull me back on to the road. My brothers tried to keep me awake and moving faster because it was not safe for the three of us to remain behind while everyone had gone. I tried to open my eyes but they refused to obey. All of a sudden, I left the road and hit a tree with my forehead. Everyone who was around me burst into laughter including Garang, Acien and even a five-year-old girl called Kuei Atem.

I did not go back to sleep again after I hit the tree with my forehead until we reached Bar-el-Gal River after a very long walk. That's because I had a severe headache and I was embarrassed when everyone laughed at me. That five-year-old girl inspired me to stay awake and focus on walking instead of sleeping since she was able to hold her eyes open. She was walking on her own feet without anyone carrying her. I asked myself this question: If a five year old girl is determined to stay awake, and keep walking on her own without assistance, why not me? Therefore, I found myself walking very fast, wide awake, until we arrived at the shore of Bar-el-Gal.

Chapter Five: Another Crossing

Arriving at Bar-el-Gal River, we found one thousand people resting. The River Bar-el-Gal stranded them because the bridge that people use to cross the river was bombed and broken by the warplanes that had been raiding the area for many days. A man called Tong Gechez, [Tong means pastor or priest,] led the group of people we met at Bar-el-Gal. He was not actually a clergy person, but a Catholic catechist who was traveling with his Holy Bible and prayed with the group when they rested and before they set out the next day. Sometimes Tong Gechez was called "raan Nhailic," meaning man of God. His group was so pleased with him and regarded him to be a righteous man because he preached about hope and trust in God and that no matter what kind of situation they were in, God would not abandon them. Our group and Tong Gechez's people joined together since we were all in the same condition.

We then tried to find a way to cross the river. We found four small boats, but no oars to row them. We were confused and did not know what to do. Those who knew how to swim tried to do so, but the water current was too powerful and no one was able to cross the river. We stayed by the riverbank for a while, and then Lino, who had saved us from thirst when we were in the middle of Roor Chuol Akol, helped us again.

Lino's idea was that we make a very thick, long and strong rope from the barks of the trees. Then, we would tie the rope around his waist, and he would swim across the river, while many people held the rope firmly.

He would then tie the rope on a big tree on the other side. The other end of the rope would be tied to a big tree on our side. From there five people would board the boat and start to cross the river while holding and pulling at the rope. This seemed to be a good idea, so adults made the rope and then followed Lino as he instructed them. We were successful in getting him to the other side of the river where he went and found a big tree and tied the rope around it. We did the same thing on our side. All the four boats were pushed into the water. Two people who knew how to swim very well boarded the first boat to test the system. We all knew that crossing the river could put our lives at risk.

One boat, carrying two men, was pushed into the river, and those two people started pulling on the rope as they moved across the river. Reaching the middle of the river, the force of the water current became stronger than the strength of the rope and it broke. The men were left with nothing to hold. They tried to resist the water current and were fighting with one of the strongest river currents I had ever seen. They had tried to row the boat using their hands but the boat overturned and the current of the water carried both boat and men away.

Some brave older men pushed into the water to rescue those two men but they could not even come close to them because the force of the water was so strong that they could not repel it. Thus, the rescue team ended up struggling for their own lives as they swam back to the river shore leaving the original two men to fight the water. Both fought hard to save their lives by trying to swim and one managed to get himself out of the water. But the other did not make it and the raging water carried him away for good. We were all devastated. Everyone was in silence for about five minutes. Nobody was talking; there was no movement. Our rope was gone and no one could think of what to do next. We had failed in our first attempt to cross the river and we had lost one of our men. We desperately stared at one another hopelessly, like soldiers who have suffered very heavy casualties during a war.

Despite the fact that all of us were demoralized by this incident, Tong Gechez still believed that we should not give up to trying some other ways to cross the river. He stood up with his Bible and then prayed for us and asked that the good Lord bless the soul of our brother whom we had just lost, and that the Lord would give us hope and courage always throughout our journey until we reach our final destination. "Yenaken," we all respond. This means Amen. At this point, I surely did not know what that destination might be; I was just running for my life.

Tong Gechez inspired Chief Ayiindit and he told us to make another rope, which is going to be thicker than the first one. Before Lino could swim with it across the river, Tong Gechez was asked by the chief to bless the rope. After he had prayed over the rope and blessed it, it was taken to the other side of the river and was tied to a big tree for the second time.

After the rope was successfully secured on both sides of the river, Chief Ayiidit and Deng Deng, who were our leaders, told us that they wanted to try to sail across the river this time. They jumped into a boat and the boat was pushed into the river where they grasped the rope and start pulling on it. The two leaders went carefully, slowly but surely, until they reached the other side. We all were happy for their arrival on the other side and we all clapped our hands for victory. We then lined up and began crossing the river carefully to avoid another disaster. The three boats we had were small; each boat could only carry about four to five passengers. When four people had managed to sail across and reach the other side in good condition, one of them would bring the boat for the next group. The process of crossing the river went on and on for two and a half days because there were many people and the means of transport was so inadequate. We were very tired, hungry and mentally and emotionally demoralized. A dangerous situation still faced us at Bar-el-Gal.

Wild animals such as elephants, buffaloes, rhinos, hyenas, lions, crocodiles, and many others increasingly attacked us for the two days we spent by the bank of river Bar-el Gal struggling to cross.

Bar-el-Gal was a source of water to many animals as well as sources of food to some animals. If buffaloes, for instance, are thirsty and want to come and drink, the groups of lions and hyenas will then lay in ambush in order to catch and kill for food for one or more buffaloes. So if the lions and hyenas came on the river shore before their prey and found us by the riverbank instead, they were left with no choice but to attack us because all they wanted was food to eat. Since we were food to them, the predators kept attacking us and were able to kill some of our people.

On the other hand, some animals such as elephants, rhinos and buffaloes might have felt that we were distracting them from drinking because we were on the river shore. I thought both of us might have been right. I felt that our group had a right to be on the river shore because we were trying to cross the river, not to prevent or to distract the animals from drinking water. At the same time, I felt that all the animals had a right to seek water and food as well. I think if both our group and the wild animals knew how to communicate with one another, we could have worked it out.

We finally managed to gather on the other side of the river at the evening of the third day and then resume our journey again. We walked non-stop because we had been resting for three days during the long crossing and wanted to compensate for the lost time.

Chapter Six:
When Life Gives You Lemons, Make Lemonade

That long walk without rest or sleep caused us some problems. We were not able to stand in one line, exposing us to animal attacks; many people were indeed carried away by wild animals. One could get lost if not close to someone else because the path we were traveling on was narrow and grassy, making it difficult to see the path properly at night. Some people who were having difficulties with walking for up to eleven hours without rest were left behind at the distance of three to four hours away from the main group. Sometimes, the disabled would spend the whole day away, and then join the rest of us the following day, assuming they were able to fend off animals. Sometimes the large group would rest awhile to allow the others to catch up.

After we traveled throughout the night, our leaders decided that we should take about twenty minutes' rest, and wait for those who were left behind; they arrived after an hour. As we waited, four older people started to make jokes about themselves on the river crossing; soon they had everyone around laughing. They went on entertaining us by poking fun at all of us. We found this funny, too. It really helped to laugh about the frightening ordeal. Even the quiet people joined in. I was surprised to see some people acting as if nothing had happened to us despite the circumstances we had been through.

I asked Deng Deng why the jokesters were so happy while the whole group was mourning. He honestly answered me that those folks who had everyone laughing were not happy. What they were trying to do was to accept the challenge we were facing as part of their lives. If we kept dwelling on our troubles, we would all die without reaching our destination. Giving in to negative emotions could bring on illness, he said. Deng Deng concluded that the best thing for us to do was to assume that everything would be okay and try to leave normal lives.

After everyone arrived and we all had enough rest, our groups moved on and finally slept in the forest that night. But before we could go to sleep, the earlier conversation resumed. Two guys, Madut Awen and Akot, started to sing Dinka traditional songs they learned during cultural dances when they were at their villages. Their singing was so entertaining that almost everyone was paying attention to them and moved in closer. They sang the song for about 10 minutes, and then started to dance as all of us clapped our hands. Some of us were laughing because Madut Awen was an old man and it was funny to watch him move in silly ways. Their encore was storytelling. From then on, these men entertained us on every break, always including educational and encouraging stories.

One of the stories Akot told us involved him and another man competing for a lady call Nyanbol. Akot was the lady's favorite boyfriend despite the fact that the other suitor was more handsome. Their competition went on for many years until one day when his cousin told him to give up because he was concerned that Akot would lose the fight as the competition was coming down to the wire. His reasoning was that Akot was not handsome and so he did not want him to waste his time. But Akot told his cousin that love is not only about how good looking a person is, but it also involves personalities, conduct and communication.

"Even if my competitor is handsome but his message of love is unclear, mine is more clear and appealing to her, "said Akot to his cousin." I will finally be victorious, and win her hand." Akot then told his cousin that the lady loved him more because he was honest and more loving.

He further illustrated his point with a story about some animals that were also competing for one beautiful young lady. Four animals, a cat, tiger, monkey, and fox, were vying for Awut. All were accepted by the young lady to be her boyfriends because she was very respectful and was willing to accept any one who wanted to have a relationship with her whether he was ugly, poor, rich or disabled in order to find out who really loved her. As time went by, the monkey climbed to the top of the list. Awut was very comfortable with the way the monkey presented himself to her as well as his general personality as compared to the other competitors. She spent more time with him, sparking jealousy, especially in Mr. Fox. Mr. Fox decided to embarrass the monkey in front of Awut to try to change her mind.

So he kept on checking to see whether there would be a chance for him to meet Awut in order for him to implement his plan. One day he found Awut alone. He began to speak poorly of the monkey. He told Awut that he didn't have a problem sharing her with the cat and tiger because he said he was the one who colored the cat and tiger to make them handsome. He could easily strip them of their color if he wanted.

However, Fox told Awut that his big concern was the monkey because he did not understand why Awut loved him so much. He tried to convince her that the monkey was a liar and a very ugly person with crazy eyes, dirty hands, a long tail and with a very big wound on his buttocks. After the fox has made all those allegations against his rival, he left Awut in a dilemma trying to figure out whether what Fox said about the monkey was true. Awut was finally convinced and she changed her mind, falling for the fox's story.

On the following day, the monkey visited Awut as usual and when he tried to talk to her, she refused to respond. He immediately realized that something had gone wrong and he kept on asking Awut to tell him whether someone had given her wrong information about him. But Awut would not say a word to him for more than an hour until she realized that he would never leave her alone if she didn't reveal the truth. So she finally told the monkey that the fox came to her and told her bad things about him. That led her to believe that the monkey was not the type of man she wanted to be with him for her entire life, and she asked the monkey to leave her alone.

Mr. Monkey accepted all the allegations that were made against him except being a liar. Monkey explained that God did not create him with crazy looking eyes, dirty hands, long tail, and a wound on his buttocks but he ended up that way because he was a rich man who had many cows. If these cows give birth to calves, he use to carry their calves frequently, and that was how he got his long tail. Wearing glasses at school had made his eyes look funny. Sitting on a chair during the long school hours caused the wound on his buttocks.

Awut then changed her mind again, understanding that the fox was motivated by jealousy. Now, she was convinced that the monkey was actually the right choice for her, so she ended her relationship with the other three handsome animals. Awut and the monkey finally married and lived a good life.

Akot then told us that his cousin was convinced at last to continue his relationship with Nyanbol for he had proved how determined he was to achieve his goals.

Similarly, Madut Awen was not one of the best comedians, but he was used to tell us stories, as well. One of the stories involved a man who was living by himself and kept one goat and one hyena as his livestock. He always made sure that the two animals were well separated before he went to sleep because the hyena was a rival of the goat.

One day, he received a message from his parents who were living far away from him that a very severe famine had stricken their village and they needed food. He took a sack and filled it up with corn and then planned to travel to his family, but needed to arrange for someone to tend his animals. Alas, he lived in the middle of a forest and there was no one around to help.

He decided to take all the animals along. He arrived at a riverbank where he found a small boat that could only carry two people or items so he had a dilemma. Madut Awen, the narrator of this story, then asked us to tell him how this man could cross the river. We all tried and tried, and finally a guy called Angok came up with the answer. The man needed to take the goat first, leaving the maize back with the hyena because hyenas do not eat maize. After dropping off the goat, he'd return for the hyena, but would have to take the goat back, lest the hyena gobbled it up. Then he'd take the maize across. Finally, he'd return for the goat and at last everything would be on the other side.

These stories entertained us, helped us and inspired us not to think too much about our situation but to engage our minds in trying to solve the challenges the stories posed. The entertainment provided by Akol and Madut Awen strengthened us on our journey to Ethiopia.

To continue with our exodus, we were a little bit lucky as we walked across Agar and Yorol Provinces for the next two weeks because the villagers provided us with some food to eat such as peanuts, sesame [a food similar to peanuts from which oil can be made] and sorghum. Even though these rations were meager given our large numbers, we were very much thankful for their kindness in sharing the little food they had.

They also helped us with many boats to cross bodies of water such as river Bar-el- Naam and river Yorol effectively without facing many challenges like the ones we had encountered when we were crossing river Bar-el-Gal and river Wau. They rowed the boats for us, insuring safe passage for all. Young men from these two communities escorted us to another neighboring village because they were afraid that we could easily lose our way and end up walking into the heart of another dangerous forest like Roor chuol Akol. They guided us to the river Nile, which they could not cross without a specific invitation. They gave us information about the river and the best ways to cross it, before wishing us well and heading home.

Chapter Seven: Surviving the Nile

River Nile, or "The Great River," is generally regarded as the longest river in the world at 6, 677 km and perhaps one of the most dangerous in Africa. River Nile arises in the great lake region of central Africa with the most distant source in Southern Rwanda, and flows through Tanzania, Lake Victoria in Kenya, Uganda, Southern Sudan, Ethiopia, and all the way to Egypt in North Africa. The Nile ends in a large delta that empties into the Mediterranean Sea.

I was very much concerned and nervous when we arrived at the Nile bank because of its tremendous width. There was no boat around that we could use to cross. We were all wondering how to cross this river successfully without endangering our lives. After a few minutes of wandering around, a guy named Anei Kordit, who at seven feet was the tallest among us, decided that he would walk into the water to determine its depth. We watched anxiously. Through the first section, it remained relatively shallow, reaching Anei Kordit's waist.

Wasting no time, our leader, Ayii, called everyone to a meeting. He suggested all children twelve years of age or older and tall enough to deal with the water level remain in line with the older travelers. Volunteers would carry those who are too young to cross by themselves, which included me. He asked Anei Kordit to lead the line as we marched into the Nile. We would use him to gauge how high the water might be at any given point.

As we moved out into the river, the level remained constant until we reached the middle. There the situation worsened, for the waves increased in force and carried away those children unable to resist the current. One child, Akok Ngor Kuany, stood in front of Deng Deng, when suddenly, the water carried him away. Akok Ngor, before the accident, had a small bag on his head. The bag fell and the rope holding the bag together wound around his legs. Deng Deng had me on his shoulders. From there, I saw a bubble of breath ascend from the river, but Akok Ngor didn't stand up. Deng Deng dived into the water with me still on his shoulders. When finally he stood, holding Akok in his arms, his eyes found mine, though, by that time, I had been carried far away by the swift current. Finally, an old man, Dutdit, rescued me.

After the rescue, Deng Deng came to me, putting me back on his shoulders, and we resumed our walk across the river. He apologized, explaining he'd totally forgotten he had been carrying me. Then, he promised he'd never let such a thing happen again. We resumed walking for about one hour, finally reaching the second section of the Nile. We found this part of the Nile, the actual river, to be the deepest. No one could swim across, because of the intense speed of the water current. Many hippopotamuses, crocodiles and other dangerous animals inhabited the area. Fortunately, an island separated the deep section from the final body of water. Several fishermen lived in that area. Some of them brought their fishing boats, transporting us to the island. There we waited for those still walking. By four o'clock in the afternoon, everyone successfully completed the crossing.

We thanked the islanders and told them we planned to attempt the third and final section of the river. But the islanders explained we would be unable to do so during the evening, because all the children would need to be put in boats. Otherwise, when the water rose, they would drown. Additionally, the islanders warned, it would take approximately three and one-half hours to cross the final section, which was the widest area. And, if they escorted us, their village would be in total darkness when they returned to the island.

Our leader, Ayiindit, took the villagers' advice, for we could not cross the river without their assistance. He informed them that we would sleep in their village, and then resume our journey in the morning. When

Ayiindit told us we would be spending the night on the island, I grew very excited. Tired and afraid, I was glad I didn't have to cross the river without a good night's sleep.

I had hoped to eat well that evening. Surely, the villagers would give us food. I watched the beautiful sunset, anxiously waiting to see what the villagers would bring us before night. Though we prayed for a miracle to bring us a feast, the only marvel was that we didn't die from mosquito bites.

As darkness moved over the island, we had nothing to protect ourselves, not even a mosquito net. Even though I killed twenty or more with my hands, I still received many bites. Many of us attempted to fight back by diving into the water, but the mosquitoes waited on the river's surface until we came out.

Finally, Ayiidit decided we needed to gather firewood before dark and set the woods on fire, feeding the flames with green grass, to produce smoke. The smoke would protect us from mosquitoes. So the older people, including the chief, brought firewood to start the fire. During most of the night, we managed to chase the mosquitoes away, but we were still hungry. We were so desperate; many of us broke into villagers' farms, stealing beans and maize. We knew stealing was a sin, but we did so, in order to survive. Most cooked their portions of the stolen food. Some, including me, became so hungry that we ate the food raw, which caused constipation.

One of the constipated men, his stomach extended, appeared to be critically ill. Though over forty years old, he cried out loudly, like a small child. His cries soon awoke the villagers. When they came to investigate, they realized we had stolen their crops. Some of the villagers picked up big sticks to beat us. But when they found so many of us sick, they were more sympathetic. We apologized for our sinful behavior, begging for forgiveness. The villagers accepted our apology, and, in return, asked our forgiveness for not providing us with food. They confessed they did not have enough to feed one thousand people.

One of the villagers was a medicine man, who promised to save us from constipation. After going to his house, he returned with tree roots. He instructed every sick person to bite a piece of root, chew it, and then swallow. He began with the critically ill man. As soon as the man bit the root, he vomited and quickly recovered. After the medicine man treated the rest of us, all the villagers returned to their homes, but we remained outside where we spent the rest of the night fighting mosquitoes.

The next morning, the villagers put all the children in our group in their boats as the adults walked, traveling through the final section of the Nile. Four hours later, we reached dry land. Grateful for their help, we thanked the villagers and wished them a safe journey back over the wide and scary Nile. All of us stood and waved good-bye. We watched until the boats vanished from our sight.

Chapter Eight:
On to the Sahara

After the villagers left, we rested on dry land for some time before we moved on, traveling on foot for several days. Finally, before sunset, we arrived at a place named Mach Deng. This town contained many houses with roofs made of white sheets of iron. Such houses were clearly visible to Sudanese regime warplanes, so bombings were frequent. The Sudanese government planned to kill all those living there, simply because they were southerners. In that town, I witnessed many holes caused by bombs.

When we arrived, Kuol Manyang Juk, the person in charge of Mach Deng, requested we leave there as soon as possible. He said Khartoum warplanes would soon be coming to bomb the town. After listening to his advice, we quickly decided to leave, as we realized what disastrous consequences would result if we did not do so. Unfortunately, before we started our journey, we heard the drone of incoming planes, followed by the loud sounds of exploding bombs. The multiple bombs left many of us dead and others wounded. My two brothers and I were among the lucky ones, for we were not hurt. After the bombing ended, we left at once, walking into the heart of the Bor region in the state of Jonglei, which is located in southern Sudan. We traveled four days and nights, eventually arriving at Ajakager, a village located at the border of Bor.

While there, because the villagers advised us to do so, we decided to rest for a while, before moving on again. According to them, the temperature in the Sahara Desert rose to 130 degrees during the day, and then fell to fifty degrees at night, so we wisely spent the day resting shadows of trees, a cool, safe place where we hid from the pilots warplanes.

When evening approached, we drank as much water as we could hold and also filled up small containers so we could carry the precious water with us into the Sahara. Traveling through the night, we arrived at Mach Abul, which had once been a village. Before we arrived, the villagers had already migrated because of drought and unbearable weather conditions, common in the middle of the Sahara Desert. Unfortunately, the only house remaining in that deserted place had a roof made of white sheets of iron.

After resting during the day, we started out again, covering as many miles as possible before the sun rose, baking the desert.

As we journeyed, we reached a big tree. The villagers of Ajakager believed the tree to be evil, because, even in the middle of the desert, the leaves remained green throughout all seasons. Though the tree provided nice shade, we'd been told that if anyone dared to rest there, the person would die. As our group moved closer to the tree, I saw human bones under it. I was quite exhausted and thirsty, but did not go to the tree. Some of the men in our group did. Though I avoided the tree because it frightened me, I remained determined to fight the terrible situation facing me up until the last minute of my journey. On the second day, we kept moving without water or food. Before long, the desert became very hot. Desperate to quench our thirst, we urinated in our hands, drinking the tiny amount our bodies produced. Then, each of us rested and traveled alone, for we were all too exhausted to take care of anyone's needs, not even our own.

At one point, while in the middle of the Sahara Desert, I faced the worst situation I'd encountered since fleeing our village more than two months before. An elderly man threatened me, demanding that I urinate in his hands so he could drink. I explained that I'd already used what little urine I'd been able to produce for myself. The man threatened to kill me if I did not do as he instructed. He grabbed me by my throat and raised me up. Before he smashed me down to the ground, Deng Deng, my close friend, shouted, telling him to let me go. When he did not obey, Deng Deng rushed to us and took me from the man's hands. He put me on the ground and I began coughing because I found breathing difficult. Finally, my breathing returned to normal. From then on, I always followed Deng Deng for my own safety.

We moved on through the hot desert, because we found nowhere to rest and because we feared some of us would die if we stopped walking. Eventually, as we traveled, we saw many birds landing from the sky ahead of us. We took the birds to be a positive sign. As we drew closer, we saw an oasis. Excited by the prospect of water, all of us ran. When, finally, we came to the oasis, we discovered buffaloes and other animals had already drunk all the water. Since only stagnant mud remained, we were left with no choice except to eat the gooey mess to moisten our parched throats and fill our hungry stomachs. Despite eating huge amounts, we still remained thirsty. As we lay down, waiting for death, I saw a small cloud forming above our heads. Finally, rain came, filling the oasis once again. We drank much of it, then filled our containers, which made it possible to travel across the desert until we arrived at Gumuro village during the night. The following morning, after being counted, we realized hundreds of our people had not made it through the desert. Hurting over the tremendous loss, we grieved.

Chapter Nine: Ethiopia

After resting at Gumuro, we resumed our journey. Traveling for three days, we arrived at the River Pinyudo in Ethiopia. When we arrived on the banks there, the villagers standing on the other side saw us and crossed over. They talked to us, but we were unable to understand what they were saying. They spoke in Amaric and Anyuak, languages unfamiliar to all of us. We spent time attempting to communicate with them without success until Chief Ayiin used nonverbal language, such as signals and gestures. In this way, he communicated to them that we were from Sudan, and that we had fled our country because of civil war. He asked if we could enter their country as refugees.

Finally understanding us, they agreed to let us go there, and even offered to help us cross the river. Our own leader cautioned us to wait until everyone had safely arrived before continuing to walk toward Ethiopia.

When everyone made it to the other side, we moved on, passing by the town near the river, where children and even some adults laughed at us because we walked naked. Most of our clothes had been torn from our bodies by trees. They also laughed at us because we had lost so much weight. My own head appeared too big for my body and I could count my bones. Those who had sympathy for us, cried. Some of the children mocked us; others followed, shouting Ajuil Marach, which in Anyuok meant bad homeless people.

Ignoring the villagers' insults, we kept moving without responding to anything. Finally we cleared the unfriendly village, arriving at the streets of Pinyundo town.

While walking, we picked up grains which had fallen to the ground. After we passed through Pinyundo, we found a trash area where the residue of local Ethiopian liquor called Daagim had been dumped. Even a half mile before we came to the dump, I noticed the smell of Daagim and all of us raced for the trash. Once there, we enjoyed our dinner in the trash area.

An Ethiopia government official moved us from the trash area to a grassy area before bringing in two trucks filled with many sacks of maize and firewood. They told us to take the food and eat it. Our leader thanked them for their help and we divided the food and cooked it. This was our first full meal in the three months since we fled from our country. After we ate, we decided to sleep right there.

Early the next morning before we could get up and hit the road again, the same official who had provided us with the food told our chief Ayiindit that they had communicated with their president who had told them to let us remain in Pinyundo until further notice. The Ethiopian president informed Dr. John Garang, the SPLA leader, about our arrival at Pinyudo.

SPLA was comprised of a group of students, policemen, soldiers and older people from southern Sudan and marginalized areas who had fled Sudan and gone to Ethiopia in 1982 and 1983 before the destruction of 1987. SPLA rebelled against the government because they were targeted and were unjustly killed every day. These groups of angry Southerners formed the SPLA party under Garang's leadership in order to represent those who were suffering. Garang was very much concerned about our situation at Pinyudo when he had learned that we were unaccompanied minors. He decided to send someone from his group to be our leader.

Two days later, Ethiopian government officials came back with a man called Pieng Deng Kuol (Majok) who was Garang's choice. He was living in Pinyundo town before our arrival there, as a representative of the Sudanese people. He was about twenty eight to thirty years of age at the time. Garang had appointed him because of his leadership experience and skills. He had acquired these qualities from his father Deng Kuol (Majok), who was a chief/leader and a ruler of the Abyei people. Abyei is one of the places in southern

Sudan where civil war had intensified because of the oil and minerals there. Deng Kuol had more than seventy wives and more than one hundred and fifty children. This taught his son Pieng Deng to be a good decision maker who was generous, kind and caring for many people.

Mr. Pieng and the Ethiopian officials told us that Pinyundo would be our destination. Pieng Deng then brought his belongings and told us that he was going to live with us under the trees in the bush. He said he had been put in charge of all of us because he could communicate with Ethiopian people very well through the English language. Before that day ended, Mr. Pieng stepped up as our new leader. He had many different ideas such as the clearing of the tall grasses we had been sleeping on under the trees. Respectfully, we accepted his plan and began to clear out the grasses.

While we were cleaning our sleeping area, most of us were severely burned or cut by the grasses. Many were bitten by snakes or spiders or stung by scorpions. Some started to die from the injuries from these wild animals and insects. In spite of this, we managed to clean out the thick foliage a little bit and were able to find a small resting spot that allowed us to sleep better than since we fled our country. Every day after that, we cleared more grass under the trees, because our number was growing.

We spent one month sleeping under trees while Ethiopian people provided us with food and from them, some of our people heard that there were training bases for the SPLA. The Ethiopians said that the SPLA was recruiting southerners who were twenty years of age and above and interested in becoming soldiers. When those of us who were eight years or older heard this news, many hoped to go join the SPLA in those military training bases. The older ones decided to leave at night while we were sleeping. Even the adults who had suffered with us throughout our journey, including Garang, decided to leave us too. Ultimately, Garang completed his military training and then fought against our enemy. Later, we learned that he was killed in action.

This left just us children who later became 'the lost boys and girls of Sudan' alone that night, not because they didn't care about us, but because they were willing to sacrifice their lives in order to train as soldiers. They wanted to regain their land, children and wives they had lost to the enemy in southern Sudan.

Many of us slept comfortably that night without knowing what was going on and when we woke up the following morning, we found out that all the adults had left. When we learned this, we all cried because we had lost our second parents who had been so dear and helpful to us as we walked together from our villages all the way to Ethiopia. They had always been there to help us. Even during wild animal attacks, the older people made sure that all of us were well protected. If we happened to find something to eat or drink, the adults made sure that the children ate and drank first. Our elders had been our last hope and when we learned that morning they were no longer with us, we were all shocked and devastated. We decided that they must have abandoned us because we were a burden to them.

While we were crying, Mr. Pieng Deng called us into a meeting. He assured us that the people who had joined the SPLA training did not leave us because they were tired of us but they left us because we were too young to be trained as soldiers. Most of us were under the age of ten. I raised my hand to tell Pieng that I was willing to go with Deng and my older brother Garang anywhere they might go because I loved them so much and that they were the only parents God left to me. Mr. Pieng replied very kindly that all of us were to be like brothers, sisters, mothers and fathers to one another. He said that we would stick together and face whatever came as one spirit, one mind and one body. Moreover, he promised us that he would take good care of us and try very hard to find additional mature Sudanese people to help tend to our needs. Pieng told us to go back to our shelters to find food to eat and move on with life.

Our number grew larger every day as people kept coming to join us in Pinyundo. Later, the number of lost boys and girls of Sudan reached almost twenty thousands and occupied the part of town that was called the Pinyundo refugee camp.

With so large a number of refugees, the Ethiopian government became unable to feed us any longer, and they reported our presence in their territory to United Nations High Commissions for the Refugee (UNHCR). UNHCR sent a team of Ethiopian people to assess the situation. When the team arrived, most of them started to cry because they could hardly believe that they found children at the age of seven years and above whose bodies were nothing but bones, who were dying or burying their own brothers and sisters, and were living alone under trees without parents. The team gave us the food they had brought before going back to Addis Ababa, the capital of Ethiopia, to report our condition to UNHCR headquarters in New York.

A few weeks later, Pieng Deng received a message from Addis Ababa saying that a UNHCR team would be bringing an American congressman to visit us. He was very pleased to hear this and held a meeting to brief the adults who had recently arrived from Sudan. After the meeting, Pieng Deng and the adults called a general meeting for all the lost boys and girls. After he told us about the visit of the congressman and UNHCR, one of the adults told us that he would teach us a song in English to welcome our visitors.

Before the meeting ended, we began to learn the song. It went like this: "Welcome, welcome American congressman, welcome, welcome UNHCR" and so forth. This seems pretty easy to me nowadays but it was very difficult to learn at the time I first heard the song. Those were the first English words I learned and words like UNHCR were very hard for me to pronounce. I used to call it UNIC Thiar, which was totally irrelevant to the UNHCR. I had translated the acronym of UNHCR into my own language using my own point of reference. "UNIC Thiar" was my understanding of UNHCR in Dinka. If one were to translate my phrase of UNIC Thiar into English, it means that there are ten United Nations High Commissioners for the Refugee (UNHCR) worldwide.

After we repeated the song several times, the meeting ended and we promised to practice the song for three days so that we could sing it well when the visitors arrived. The night before the next rehearsal, I tried to test myself as I had decided to memorize the song so I could sing it without asking anyone for help. But I could only pronounce a few words such as welcome, welcome, American congressman and continued to struggle with the pronunciation of UNHCR. I tried and tried to remember UNHCR but I couldn't, so I gave up and went to sleep. The following morning, we were called out to go back to the meeting place where we rehearsed the song for about two hours before we dispersed to find some food.

By the time we had practiced the song for two more days, we were able to sing it by ourselves even during our free time. I was very excited to be able to sing the song because I was interested in learning foreign languages and I thought I had learned to speak English since I could sing the song.

On the fourth day, the visitors arrived at the meeting place around 10:00 in the morning and we sang the welcoming song. Being short, I was not able to see any of the visitors until the song ended and we were asked to sit down to listen to the UNHCR speech as well as the speech from the American congressman.

When everyone had sat down, my comrades and I were able to see clearly our visitors for the first time. This was the first time we had ever seen any white men. I thought I might have dreamed what I was seeing and closed my eyes for a moment. When I opened my eyes again, I still saw the same people. One of the white men started to talk to us in English and it was translated to us in Dinka. I was a very nervous and frightened seven-year-old because I thought the congressman who was addressing us was a ghost and might kill us later. This is because I had thought we were the only humans who existed in the world. We were all waiting anxiously for the meeting to end so that we could go and touch the white men in order to feel their skin with our hands.

The congressman and UNHCR staff spoke for about thirty minutes. The congressman promised us that the American people were going to provide us with food and that we would be protected under the international law just as other refugees are sheltered worldwide.

As soon as the meeting was over, I tried to go and touch either the congressman or one of the other three white men, but I did not succeed because we were more than twenty thousand people who were all trying to touch one of these four white men. The visitors left after they spoke and greeted us.

Everyone else wanted to touch the white men, too. As a result of the fight to make contact, most of us were pushed down on the ground and many people were walked on or seriously injured. Ethiopian nurses who had attended the meeting treated minor injuries on the spot. Those who were seriously injured were taken to the hospital in Gambella for further intensive treatment. After things quieted down, a friend told me he had touched one of the white men and that his skin was just a normal skin like ours. I was convinced that our world is made up of people who have different skin colors. I realized that white men were ordinary people like us and not ghosts.

Chapter 10: Forming a Family

We spent some days without food after the UNHCR and congressman visited. Finally, we received some maize grains, beans, oil, bed sheets, and clothes. The food and clothes we received from UNHCR were in sacks, tins, and bags stamped with USA. Those lost boys who were twelve years old or older, together with the few adults who were our caretakers, were asked by Pieng Deng to help unload the trucks that were carrying these supplies.

When they finished, Pieng Deng told our caretakers to help put all of us into groups. Pieng and his team managed to put all twenty thousand children into twelve groups. Each group consisted of more than thousand lost boys and girls with many subgroups.

Pieng Deng then divided the five hundred to six hundred caretakers into twelve groups and assigned each with responsibility for a group of children. The caretakers were adults, mostly men, from ages twenty five to forty who arrived from Sudan after our previous guardians joined the military. Some of them were unable to join the military due to sickness. After they recovered, they volunteered to help us. Pieng Deng, together with our caretakers, appointed some of the boys who were fourteen years and above to help lead.

Then he called the leaders of each group together to give out our share of food and clothes. We were able to eat well, cover ourselves and had bed sheets to use for the first time since we fled our homeland. We slept well that night because we all had blankets to spread on the ground and the bed sheets to cover ourselves. We could now protect ourselves from cold and had other things that we had not had for a long time. We were all glad and very appreciative to American people and the rest of the world who were contributing their money, time, and prayers for our sake.

The following morning, Pieng Deng, who had now become the father of so many, toured each group and held meetings. Our group was the fourth one. He told us that each one of us was a brother/sister to those who were living in our group and he insisted that we needed to live with one another in a peaceful manner. He also said that we needed to take care of one another if anyone got sick or attacked by a wild animal.

We knew his advice was very important and we began to accept one another and try to live as one family. But it was not easy for us to live with together because we were all children and we ended up fighting among ourselves. When Pieng Deng saw there were a lot of problems, he decided to mix all the twelve groups twice a month to help the children know themselves as one family and live with one another in harmony. His plan worked well. We were able to get to know everyone all over Pinyundo and we learned to live with one another like children who share a mother and father.

Despite the fact that we were given enough food, clothes, bed sheets and blankets, we were still surrounded by many problems. The first was how to cook the food. Most of us did not know how to cook because we were all so young and were too small to cook with a big saucepan or in a big container to feed more than fifty people. In addition, it is our Dinka traditional way of life that males were not allowed to learn how to cook. All duties that are performed in southern Sudan are generally divided according to gender and cooking is considered the duty of females. Male duties, beginning with young boys, were taking care of the livestock, growing crops, and similar chores.

But this fact did not prevent us from learning how to cook for ourselves. Boys ten years and above were selected to be the ones cooking. Within each main group of boys, each subgroup contained about fifty boys. So about five boys were to cook two meals for their group one day and another group of five boys would cook the next day.

The children who were too young to cook went to the nearby forest to collect firewood or to the river to fetch cooking water. I helped with these tasks. We did our duties on an alternating basis also. If I collected firewood today, then it would be my turn tomorrow to go to the river with some other boys and fetch water for cooking.

Those boys who cooked for us with the help of caretakers tried hard to do it well. However, their meals often brought on illness because the food was not cooked well, and many of us had diarrhea, vomiting, and some died as a result of poor cooking.

Some of us at the Pinyundo refugee camp who collected firewood and fetched water lost their lives through wild animal attacks in the forest and in the river. Sometimes the boys who fetched water for cooking would decide to play in the water for a while before they returned to camp. While they were playing, crocodiles could attack them and kill or harm them. The water current washed some away because the river flooded if even a small rain came. One time I was playing in a shallow part of the river Pinyundo. Then rain came, filling it quickly. I was lucky to be saved by one of the Ethiopian villagers who saw me struggle for my life. He threw himself into the water and got me out, but my friends were washed away.

On top of these difficulties, we had insufficient cooking materials. Each group of 50 boys was given one big saucepan and one medium saucepan for cooking both broth and food. Those two saucepans could not hold enough food for 50 boys at one time. So those five boys had to cook more than two times for each meal and they were forced to find dishes to empty the first batch into and make more food. We did not have enough dishes, so we would cut a maize sack and make it look like bed sheet or blanket and then we would empty the food that was in the saucepan onto the sack and make another batch until there was enough food for everyone. After the food was ready to eat, a group of 10 boys sat on each sack that contained the prepared food and shared the food together as one family. So sharing is one of the qualities that we, the lost boys of Sudan, all have in common.

Another problem we were facing was shelter. We had food to eat at Pinyundo camp, but we were living under trees. We did not have houses and it was raining constantly. Rain water was all over our sleeping areas, mosquitoes bred rapidly in the surrounding areas, snakes bit every day and night, scorpions stung, and lions, hyena and some other wild animals attacked us. Recognizing these threats, our camp leader, Pieng Deng, decided that we needed to build houses in order to protect ourselves from the elements. After he met with our caretakers and told them about the plan for building houses, his idea was well received.

After we were all told about the construction plan, we divided our main group of twelve boys into three groups, with each group assigned a different duty in building the houses. The first group was sent to another forest called Teda to cut down trees that would be used as long poles and short poles for building the houses. The Teda forest was actually was about three hours away from the Pinyundo refugee camp, so the older boys, who were more able to cut trees, were the first sent to Teda. Because this was such a large task, as many poles were needed to build our houses, these boys remained at Teda for some weeks. After the first group had gathered enough poles to build houses for all twenty thousand plus boys, the next group was sent to Teda to carry all the long and short poles on their shoulders while walking the whole three miles back to camp. It took two to three boys to carry each long pole because the poles were too heavy for just one boy to carry by himself.

The second group was sent to a place called Pal Wak to gather grasses that could be used for roofing. Like the first group that was at Teda, this group would stay several weeks at Pal Wak. Some of the boys would cut enough grasses to produce many bundles and some of the boys would help carry the bundles back to our camp.

The third and final group was sent to a place called Pan John Umot to gather ropes that would be used in tying the poles and grasses onto the roofs of the houses since we did not have nails and other building materials. One month later, after we had transported all the building materials into the camp, we started marking and clearing the ground where the houses were going to be built. Then, we began to dig the many holes needed for all the short poles. When all the short poles were in place, in order for them to stand firm, we filled the holes up with the mud that we had already dug out of the holes.

After that, the tallest boys would climb up on the short poles and tie the long poles to the short poles. By tying all the long poles together on one big long pole, the house would finally have a roof. Lastly, the grasses would be spread on the roof and tied down using the ropes.

There were many problems while building our houses. Many of us had cut our hands and legs while trying to cut down trees. Some boys even cut their fingers off while they were cutting grasses and ropes. Others fell down into branches while they were cutting long and short poles.

I still remember one incident when one of the boys in our group, called Deng Mel, fell down while cutting a tree and broke his leg. He was brought back to us and from there sent to Addis Ababa, where his leg was treated. He later returned to us after he healed.

Although there were various challenges, we were able to build many houses through hard work, determination, group commitment and working together as one body. All our work paid off and we were able to live in shelters where we could protect ourselves from rain, insects, and wild animals.

Chapter 11: Bringing Literacy to the Lost Boys and Girls

After we had finished building our shelters and were receiving food from UNHCR, our leader, Pieng Deng, was very concerned about how he could introduce us to learning. He wanted us to be educated, be able to read and write, have a better understanding of the world we lived in and for us to have the ability to communicate with the entire world. For most of us in the camp, our parents came from a background of illiteracy and thus ninety nine percent of the lost children were unschooled as well. You could say that our illiteracy was something that all of us had inherited from our great, great grandparents.

Our great grandparents did not have any education because southerners and many indigenous people of Sudan were denied education by the Sudanese government. This government was widely controlled by the Arabs who are in the north and who have been ruling the country for many decades. There were few schools built in the south and marginal areas. The few that did exist were mainly for those Arab children whose parents were living in the south and also for the few southerners who were lucky enough to work in a government job. Even if the southerners who had no position in the government wanted to put their children in school, their children would not be permitted to attend. Or sometimes, southern parents would be asked to pay much more money for tuition compared to the amount northern parents paid.

For instance, in our family there were thirteen children. Seven children are my stepbrothers and stepsisters, and five others are my full siblings. I remember the time when my family went to a school that was near our village in a town called Araith and asked the school administration if they would allow us to be enrolled. Our father was asked to pay an amount of money that he could not afford. So when our father saw that there was no way for him to put all of us in school, he sold about ten cows to be able to put just one of my elder brothers in school. The rest of us just stayed at home.

The few of the native Sudanese who were lucky to have a little education were those who were taught by missionaries, such as the Comboni missionaries and other missionaries who have been very helpful to the people of Sudan as a whole. Most who attended the missionary schools were basically taught in English, which was the main subject in the school, followed by Arabic. Those in public schools learned Arabic as the main subject for the entire length of their education.

With that background in mind, Mr. Pieng Deng held a meeting with all our caretakers and told them that he would like all the lost boys and girls to engage in some activities that would keep us busy so that we would be able to cope with the bad conditions that were facing us. One of the activities he suggested to our caretakers was school. Pieng Deng insisted to the caretakers that not only would teaching us help us in the short term, but school would also prepare us for a better future wherever we were going to end up. He stated that the idea of opening learning places for twenty thousand children was a worthwhile pursuit, but he was not sure where he could find people who knew how to read and write and who would be willing to volunteer to help. When he finished his speech, all the caretakers were very pleased with his idea of educating us. In fact, most of them volunteered to be our teachers because many had been students in missionary schools in southern Sudan.

They had fled the country because the Sudanese government had destroyed their schools during the general destruction. The administration claimed that the students were the supporters of the Sudan People's Liberation Movement, which rebelled against the government's cruelty and injustices against the innocent natives. Pieng Deng became very excited about the support that he received from our caretakers. He sent them back to us and they briefed us about the school program. We were all excited too because we were in need of something new and interesting.

The following morning, all the lost boys and girls were assembled in one place. Pieng Deng and our caretakers asked us to start clearing grasses out under many big trees near our camp. After two busy days of hard work, we were able to prepare a very large area near each group's home.

The next morning, each of the twelve groups was called out to the site. Each was further divided into many subsets and told to go under a given tree. Each group under a tree made up a class of pupils. And so our school was established under the trees.

Each class was made up of approximately fifty students and two teachers. One teacher was an English teacher and another was a mathematics teacher.

We were not taught the first day of school because all of our teachers/caretakers were busy trying to organize us. After they organized the twelve groups into different classes of pupils, each class was to be registered.

Our class registration was conducted by Mario ring Mathok. He came to our class while we were sitting under the trees and told us that he was going to be our English teacher, which meant that he was also our class master. Anything to do with the class affairs such as registration, making the class's final exam report and handling any disputes between the students was his responsibility first before he could forward problems to the school administration. After our teacher Mario introduced himself to us, he then requested that we make one line for the registration process. He registered every one of us successfully without any trouble. We were all told to go back and come to school the next day to begin learning.

We went back to our group very excited. We were talking to one another about the opening of the schools throughout that evening and night as each of us waited anxiously for the next day to come. We went to bed that night with hopes that the big day would come within two hours of sleeping.

When the first cock crowed, or around 4:00 a.m., one of my roommates, called Wol, woke up from sleep and started to wake all of us up in order to brush our teeth and get ready for class. When I woke up and opened the door to see outside, I noticed that it was still dark. So I asked Wol to stop waking everyone up because it was still night and the wild animals might attack us if we went outside in the dark.

The rest of my roommates listened to my advice and went back to sleep. But Wol did not go back to sleep. He told me that he had finished sleeping and he insisted that it was time for him to go to class and begin to learn something new in his life. I did not argue with him because I was feeling the same way. I, too, wished to see the darkness passing very quickly so that I could go to class during the day and begin to learn.

I went back to sleep with my other roommates and got up when 6:00 finally rolled around. We brushed our teeth, using toothbrushes made from small tree branches, and washed our faces, legs and arms with river water only; there was no soap. Since we had no combs, there wasn't much we could do with our hair. When we were done, we headed to our schools.

The entire school was assembled in one place before we would break to our separate classes. One of the caretakers who was our school headmaster told us that we would be assembling every day for a school update before going to our respective classes.

When the headmaster finished addressing the school, he told us to disperse to our classes. My classmates and I went to our class under the tree, and all of us sat down and waited quietly for our English teacher to arrive. About three minutes later, Mr. Mario came to us and we all stood up as a sign of respect to him. He greeted us, "Saba el kher," followed by a nice smile on his face. We responded back to him, "Saba el Noor Uztash." This is a morning greeting in Arabic that means "good morning, good morning teacher." After exchanging greetings, he asked us to be seated.

He told us that he was going to be calling roll and he needed each one of us to respond to him "Naam" when we heard our name. "Naam" is an Arabic word for yes. He told us that all of us who were registered the prior day had shown up for the class period. He encouraged all of us to always come to class and learn what we did not know from him and the other teachers.

After some words of encouragement, he told us that it was time for him to give us his first lesson and he begged us to pay much attention and cooperate with him. During teacher Mario's first English lesson the first word he taught us was good followed by morning teacher and "yes." He kept singing the four words and the whole class repeated the words many times after him until we were able to say them correctly. When his time for the day in the class was over, he told us to keep memorizing the words at home so that we would be able to say them correctly tomorrow during class. That was his last comment for the day and he left us under tree waiting for the mathematics teacher to arrive.

Our mathematics teacher, Maker, received the same respectful treatment from us and also greeted us the same way that our English teacher had. The distinction between mathematics and English teachers was that mathematics teacher did not have to attend to anything first, such as roll call, before he began teaching. The other thing that was different was their teaching techniques.

Instead of letting the class learn mathematics by singing a song as Mr. Mario did during English period, Mr. Maker told each one of us to go to nearby trees and bring five small sticks back to class. When we came back with the sticks, he told us to make a big circle. After we formed the circle, he began to walk around the circle and wrote five numbers down on the ground. He asked each one of us to try and write the numbers down on our own. We kept trying to write the numerals one to five while he moved around the circle helping us write the numbers correctly.

We kept practicing for about an hour until he told us to stop writing. He began to read out the numbers that we had written on the ground, starting from number one. We repeated the word "one" after him. Then he told us that his teaching time was over and it was time for us to go home. He promised that even though the numbers might have been difficult for us to write or pronounce, it would become easier as we practiced and continued learning. He encouraged us and told us we should not be dismayed or quit coming to school because of things that we did not understand. He assured us that we would understand everything as time went by because "practice makes perfect," he said.

When I heard his advice, I felt relieved because I was very worried and concerned about the fact that I was not able to write "Three" and "Five" correctly during the first mathematics lesson of my entire life. I thought I would never be able to write these two numbers. But since teacher Maker encouraged us and told us that we will be able to learn things that were hard for us to understand the first time, it helped me build back my confidence that I was going to learn English and mathematics no matter what happened as I went down the road with my studies.

After we were all sent back to our houses after the second lesson period was over around noon, I went straight to our house and began to ask my roommates about what they had learned in their classes. I found out that many of us in different classes had learned different things the first day of school. I spent the first day trying to memorize all that I had learned in my English and mathematics classes.

When I returned to school the next day, I found out that all I learned the previous day had evaporated out of my mind. But I did not worry this time because I knew learning new things is a process and that I needed to be patient and keep going, even if I had forgotten what I learned yesterday.

Days and months went by as we were all learning English and mathematics under the trees without any books or supplies. Rain could interrupt our learning and sometimes we would stay in our house for two to three days without going to school if there were non-stop rain in the camp.

So when the camp leader, Mr. Pieng Deng, had enough of the rain delays, he ordered the school to close temporarily and told all the lost boys and the care takers/teachers to build classrooms. We took the same steps we had taken when we built our houses, and three months later, we were able to build twelve school buildings in the Pinyundo refugee camp. After the classrooms were built, Pieng Deng reopened the school and all of us were able to learn once again, in much improved surroundings.

Although we now had indoor classrooms, we still went outside to make a big circle in front of our classroom where we could practice writing the English letters and mathematics numbers on the ground. This was because our teachers had no blackboards to write the lessons on and we had no exercise books to write in. So, what we usually did was that the teacher taught the pronunciations of the alphabetical letters or counting of numbers in the classroom and then the students would go outside to practice.

A couple of months passed and a group of UNHCR delegates came to visit Pinyundo to see our living situation. Pieng Deng took the delegates to the schools for a tour. The delegates realized that we were learning without standard supplies, such as books, notebooks, pencils, pens, blackboards, and chalk and their team leader promised Mr. Pieng that he would present our needs to the UNHCR general assembly. While assessing the situation of the camp and the schools, the UN delegation took our photos and videotaped us writing on the floor with our hands and singing welcoming songs in Arabic and Dinka.

About a month and half later, all twelve schools received some blackboards and chalk, first grade textbooks, notebooks, pens, pencils and pencil sharpeners. Each classroom was given one blackboard and a few boxes of chalk, which were kept in the teacher's office. Each teacher would take one piece of chalk with him to the class and return what was left of the chalk to use for the next day's lesson. Each teacher also was given one ink pen for marking the roll call and the students' assignments and half of a pencil in case his/her pen ran out of ink.

For the students, one notebook was divided into three parts and one part was given to each of us. In the writing book, one side was used for English and the other side for math. The pencils were cut in half and distributed. One small sharpener was to be shared by almost forty students. Each child received one-half of a ruler. There weren't enough textbooks for everyone, so the teachers kept them. After the distribution of the learning materials, the day was over and we went home.

When we went back to school the next morning, I tried to write my two subjects in my writing notebook, but I was not able to write the letters and numbers in a straight line because I did not know how to hold a pencil or how to write in the notebook.

When the teacher left the class, I went to check with my classmates to see how they were doing with their writing. I found that the whole class was having the same problem and I was reminded that it was not easy for us to immediately learn what was new to us. Despite the bad conditions we were in, we continued to learn in Pinyundo day after day, week after week, month after month, and year after year with the hope that tomorrow would be a better day.

Chapter 12: Playing Just as Children Should

Usually after the school day ended, we participated in recreational activities. We would go home and try to cook or find something to eat. Then, we would go find a place to play and something to play with. Most of us participated in sporting activities, such as soccer, volleyball, basketball and racing. I was in the group of lost boys who liked to play soccer.

Unfortunately, the type of soccer balls, volleyballs, and basketballs we played with were not real balls inflated with air. We used to go to an open area with a pumpkin or calabash, separate ourselves into two groups, and draw a line between the open areas. Each group was to prevent the other group from crossing the line in the middle while they had possession of the "ball." We would play either by kicking the makeshift ball with our bare feet or by passing it to our teammates with our hands. We ran around carrying the pumpkin for a short time because it would hurt our feet when we kicked it. It hurt so badly that some of us would quit before the playing time was over and we would have to stop for the day.

We played with a pumpkin for many days until some of the older boys who had a clue what a ball was supposed to look like decided to try to make one. Samuel Lueth, a group leader, collected some pieces of clothing. He then used rope to tie all the different items together until it become a big round object and started to kick that object with some of his friends. The next day he made a few more for his group.

As time went by, all twelve groups of lost boys and girls stopped playing with pumpkins and calabashes and played with a sock ball, or one made out of pieces of clothes or ropes. We used the sock balls as soccer balls, volleyballs, and basketballs. After a time playing with the sock ball with no air, we even were able to make some sock balls that could be inflated.

The UN had established a medical clinic in the camp and we went to the trash area and collected the rubber gloves used by the nurses. We breathed into the gloves without washing them first and tied the mouth of the glove tightly with rope. Then we put the inflated glove in a sock or wrapped pieces of clothing around the glove until the glove looked like a round ball and was ready to be play.

The glove sock balls were better than the ones made from clothing. The glove sock ball had air in it and it was less dense than our first efforts. However, one of the disadvantages was that it could burst easily if two players' feet hit it at the same time. Another disadvantage was that if the ball was kicked into the thorns it would be pierced and deflated, ending play prematurely. So, we usually took with us some normal sock balls to the playing areas and used them when the glove sock balls were punctured.

Five months after we began playing with the sock and glove balls, another team of UN delegates visited our refugee camp and saw the open areas filled with twelve groups of children playing soccer, volleyball, and basketball, which had impressed them. Since the visitors had to spend some time with us in the camp, our caretakers decided to organize a tournament so that the UN staff could get a good sense of our sports programs.

The first time I participated in a soccer tournament I honestly didn't play very well because I was very nervous. I was afraid of our opponents and distracted by all the yelling and cheering of our supporters in the crowd. If the ball was kicked or passed to me by a teammate, some supporters would start jeering at me before I could even get possession of the ball. Then I lost focus and all kinds of thoughts raced through my mind about what I should ultimately do with the ball, when I actually had control of it.

Frankly speaking, I was sometimes not able to control the ball or pass it to a teammate. I kept losing control of the ball because the fans magnified my existing fear. I was not very comfortable playing during the first half of the game, and when it ended, I told our coach Goup Chol that I was not going to play in the second half. Goup Chol advised me that I needed to concentrate and focus only on the game and not worry about anything beyond the field of play. He assured me that I would see some changes in my game if I would take his advice and play the second half. All he wanted was for me and the entire team to go back on the field and have fun and enjoy ourselves as we usually did during our practice sessions.

I was really touched by the advice Goup Chol had given us and my courage returned. When the referee blew the whistle for the second half, I was the first one on my team to walk on the field. Soon after the second-half kickoff, I discovered that I was actually playing well: I could control the ball and pass accurately to my teammates. In fact, the entire team was playing better than before. The fans were pleased too, and suddenly started cheering our team.

When I scored the first goal of the match, my teammates rushed onto the field and hugged me, their faces covered with tears of joy. Toward the end of the game, my teammate Bol Manyuol scored a second goal and gave us a 2-0 lead over our opponents. Two minutes later, the game ended. Some of our team's supporters who were watching rushed onto the field and carried us on their shoulders and joined our fans in a victory celebration that lasted until midnight.

The next day we moved on to the next level in the tournament. Ultimately, our school finished the tournament in sixth place, but all our teachers, supporters and Coach Goup Chol were pleased with our performance, even though our team had not won the championship.

Our teachers/caretakers also participated in sports competitions. However, they competed in soccer, volleyball, and basketball with the Ethiopians living in the town of Pinyundo. Their competitions were more entertaining than ours because both the Ethiopians and our caretakers were very good at sports. Our caretakers were victorious most of the time.

The refugee camps for Sudanese in Pinyundo and Itang sometimes participated in tournaments. The Itang camp had many more refugees that our camp did. The distance between the Itang and Pinyundo camps was a nine to ten hour drive or a three-day walk on foot. For this reason, the tournaments were hosted in both camps. If Itang hosted one tournament, the next one was held in the Pinyundo camp. This arrangement allowed the fans of both camps to attend the competitions and support their teams.

When competition between the Pinyundo and Itang camps was introduced, I was selected for the under-ten youth soccer team. About one hundred and fifty players representing the various Pinyundo teams were going to be transported to the competition in three big trucks, the same UNHCR trucks that regularly brought food to our camp. The trucks were open at the top and had neither seats nor anything to hold onto when they traveled down rough roads. When our truck moved, all of us started to fall down on one another.

Later, as the truck picked up speed, the journey got even worse. We began to vomit on one another because the truck was shaking so much. Or maybe it was because this was the first time many of us had ever traveled in a motor vehicle. Our trip to the Itang camp took nine hours, and when we arrived, most of us became sick and were unable to walk on our own. We were carried to the houses where we were to spend the night.

Despite the carsickness, the following morning all of us were somehow able to compete in the tournament. Some of the Pinyundo teams won, and some, including my soccer team, lost. Unfortunately, at the conclusion of the competition, we had to travel back to our camp using the same trucks. Once again, the conditions were the same: everyone vomiting and falling down on one another for a grueling nine hours.

Upon our arrival at Pinyundo, everyone was standing along the road, and the whole camp was singing a song of welcome. We felt very happy for the way they all supported us. The tournaments between the Pinyundo and Itang refugee camps continued until 1990, when the new Ethiopian government expelled us from the country.

Chapter 13:
Keeping the Faith

Apart from sports, church activities were also a part of my daily life when I was at the Pinyundo refugee camp. There were three Christian denominations represented: Episcopalian, Presbyterian and Catholic. The Episcopalians met under trees near groups seven, eight, nine and ten and were led by Pastor Machar. The Presbyterians also had many members and met under a different tree. Finally the Catholics, the first denomination established in the camp, were based in group four and led by the catechists Tong Gechez, Karlo Karmic and David Amour. Most of the church activities were scheduled in the evening after the sports activities, when the weather was ideal for church members to pay attention to the word of God.

Personally, I attended Catholic services because I was born into a Catholic family. The three catechists divided up the duties in our Catholic chapel. As the senior catechist, Tong Gechez was responsible for Sunday services and morning and evening prayers; Karlo Komic sometimes assisted at either morning or evening prayers; David Amour, together with Karlo, taught hymns.

Every morning before school we would assemble for morning prayers under the appropriate tree. After we finished our sports activities in the evening, we returned to chapel to learn songs, followed by evening prayers. Sometimes I returned to my room and prayed with my roommates who attended the Episcopalian and Presbyterian churches, since I believe that message of God's love for us is present in every church. The number of people attending Christian services steadily increased because every day many more people arrived at the Pinyundo refugee camp seeking relief from the Sudanese government's destruction of its indigenous people.

Attending events such as choir practice was always interesting because I was learning wonderful songs every day and meeting new lost boys and girls who were still arriving into the Pinyudo refugee camp. One of the people that I met during choir was Nancy Abur who was two years younger than me. Nancy came with her older sister and we often played together afterwards.

Our three catechists had successfully served the Catholic chapel for six months, when Father Benjamin Madol Akol from the Rumbek diocese arrived. While we were in chapel practicing hymns one Saturday morning, Father Benjamin came and sat down in the back of the room and joined in the singing. No one among us recognized him as a priest. We all thought he was a new refugee from Sudan who had just arrived and was attracted by our singing. At the conclusion of the hymn, our choirmaster David Amour recognized Father Benjamin sitting among the people in back and ran to hug the priest. He had known Father Ben back home in Rumbek, Sudan, and shouted excitedly, "Thanks be to God Almighty for giving us Father Ben Madol!" We all were so happy because of the presence of a priest who would now take over the chapel and serve all the Catholic refugees.

The week Father Ben arrived at the Pinyundo camp attendance at Sunday services increased so dramatically that people were standing in the sun, no longer able to fit under our assigned tree. Therefore, before the service concluded, Father Benjamin and Tong Gechez announced that our chapel needed to be relocated to a place with many large trees close together, so that all church members could be accommodated.

The next day after school, some church members found a new location in the forest about twenty minutes away from our original site. We spent the next three days clearing small, thorny trees and tall grasses from the area, so that all church members could worship God together. For some months, we continued to hold chapel services at our new site under the trees. Later, we were able to build a house of worship where we could praise God, even if it was raining. In the Catholic chapel at Pinyundo, I was first a choir member and altar boy while living among the other lost boys, but later Father Benjamin took me to live at a church compound where I remained until a new government in Ethiopia expelled us.

I became very ill, even coughing up blood, and it was feared I would die. Father Benjamin took me to the church compound where I recovered. It was decided I would remain there.

Since I left my homeland, church activities had been the most important thing in my life, as well as for the other boys and girls in the refugee camps. Whenever I was thirsty during my journey to places unknown, with God's help, I was able to drink water. Whenever I was hungry, God fed me. Whenever I felt like dying, God brought me back to life. Whenever I despaired, God comforted me; whenever I was without hope, God restored my hope by showing me his kindness and love for the whole human race. That is why I chose the church's way as my path in life. All three denominations in the Pinyundo camp gave inspiration to my comrades and me. They all encouraged me with God's word, and no matter under what conditions I lived, I faced my life without fear or worry.

Chapter 14:
Illness Along the Way

One of the most serious problems we faced at the Pinyundo refugee camp in Ethiopia was disease. Many diseases thrived at the camp because of very poor sanitation and overcrowding. The camp was so congested that diseases could pass easily from one person to another. In the contaminated and stagnant water at the camp, mosquitoes could breed, and they attacked us constantly, leaving many of us sick. Among the diseases rampant at Pinyundo were diarrhea, blood dysentery, cholera, malaria, tuberculosis, anemia, mental illness and many different skin diseases.

Malaria was the most dangerous disease and killed many camp residents every day. Malaria was so widespread because the camp was located near a river where tall, thick grasses provided an ideal breeding ground for thousands of young mosquitoes. When they bit us, they spread a poison into our bodies that often resulted in death. Within the ground surrounding our dwellings, mosquitoes swarmed around natural pools of stagnant water, which provided them a further breeding place.

The mosquito attacks were virtually unstoppable because we had no mosquito nets or mosquito repellent. The only means we had to chase mosquitoes away was to set smoky fires from time to time. Roommates in each shelter would gather green grass during the day and bring it later inside. At bedtime, we would burn the grass so that we were able to sleep temporarily, before the mosquitoes attacked them once again. This type of mosquito protection was very risky, because people trying to sleep would have breathing difficulties due to a lack of oxygen in the house.

One night my roommate and I put some grass into the fire to produce smoke to keep away the mosquitoes. While we were sleeping, our house caught fire, but we were unaware of this because we lay unconscious suffering from smoke asphyxiation. Luckily, some lost boys living in a neighboring house rescued us. According to the boys, they had smelled a burning fire, and when one of them stepped outside to check, he saw our house on fire. They immediately rushed to the house and extinguished the fire with water. Then they pulled us out and laid us unconscious on the ground, where we remained for hours without any medical attention. Some of us suffered severe burns, but I had only a minor burn on my stomach. After many hours we regained consciousness and fortunately no one died. From that point on, we stopped burning a fire in our house while we are sleeping. From our experience, many others learned the lesson to never light fires indoors at night.

The second most serious diseases were diarrhea, dysentery and cholera. One of the reasons these three diseases were simultaneously so rampant in the camp was due to contaminated water. The water we used for cooking and for drinking came from the same river where every refugee washed his/her clothes and took baths. Another cause was human waste. For the first months after our arrival at Pinyundo, there were no latrines; people had to relieve themselves near the forest and then return to the living area. The accumulated waste product were exposed to flies and other insects, which flew back to camp and then contaminated our food and water. Such conditions regularly produced cholera outbreaks and caused much death among refugees in the camp. A final factor causing widespread disease was the almost constant rain in western Ethiopia, where Pinyundo camp was located. Every time it rained, the surrounding area flooded, and the floodwaters carried human waste and other contaminants into the river near camp.

When someone consumed contaminated food and water, diarrhea soon followed. Within an hour, he/she would discharge blood and mucus from the anus and sooner or later start to vomit. Because of the continuous loss of bodily fluids from diarrhea and vomiting, a person soon became dehydrated and weak. Within twenty four hours, that person would die, and we would end up going to the cemetery the next day and burying him along with ten other people who had suffered from the same condition. Such burials were a daily occurrence.

I myself suffered from malaria and diarrhea many times when I lived at the Pinyundo refugee camp. Thankfully, God protected me during my time of sickness. Even though we later dug latrines, after we had been in the camp over six months, cholera, diarrhea, and dysentery still were a major threat. We still had to use water from the contaminated Pinyundo River for cooking and drinking, and flies also continued to contaminate our food with bacteria.

The third most serious problem was mental illness. Because all of the lost boys and girls of Sudan had experienced unimaginable situations, many of us became mentally ill either during our three-month journey from Sudan, or at the refugee camp itself in Ethiopia. A major cause was that we had witnessed the destruction of our families, villages, and livestock, and the mental videotape of that horror kept replaying in our heads. Terrifying memories of the difficult trek to Ethiopia continued to haunt us. We often would dream about the attacks of wild animals we had experienced during that excruciating journey. Those who had screaming nightmares often later developed mental illness.

In addition, the living conditions in the Pinyundo camp itself contributed to poor mental health. The food we ate at the camp was not good in comparison to what we used to eat with our parents back in our homeland. Some children would become preoccupied by thoughts of home and developed the habit of refusing to eat. After two or three days of not eating or drinking water, these children would become delirious and start screaming, beating on anything nearby and throwing themselves on the hard floor. As a result of their mental state, some suffered serious bodily injuries, brain damage and even death.

A third source of widespread mental illness was that in our daily lives we all were surrounded by death. Every day our roommates, school friends and even caretakers died and we had to bury them. It is deeply disturbing for an eight, nine, or ten-year-old child to bury a human body. The image of these burials haunted many of us for months and even years. We would have nightmares about the burials and the children who passed away. Sometimes we worried that we would be the next person to die, since a best friend had died that day. Some children would become disoriented and depressed, since they had lost everyone they loved. They would just sit hopeless and alone, not allowing any of us to support and comfort them.

The mentally ill were segregated from the rest of us into their own rehabilitation center. They were a danger to us and to themselves, because they often would attack anyone nearby with a piece of metal or wood. Camp leaders together with UNHCR decided the only solution was to create a rehabilitation center where they could be given treatment for their mental problems. Some of my own relatives and friends were transferred to the rehabilitation center.

Every evening, Father Benjamin and some members of our church visited people who were seriously sick at the main clinic and at the rehabilitation center. We prayed and encouraged them to have faith that God would grant them a quick recovery. It broke my heart to see such critically ill patients, the look of agony in their eyes betraying they could soon die.

My first visit to the rehabilitation center with Father Benjamin was a frightening experience. After we had entered one of the buildings where some of the violent mentally ill children were housed, one of them, a fourteen-year old boy named Atak, managed to break the chain tied to his feet and started to attack me. Father Benjamin and I had greeted Atak as he was lying in the first bed and then had moved on to talk to other patients. Suddenly Atak came running after us and struck me on the neck with his fist. He continued to beat me, as I lay unconscious on the floor. Father Benjamin and some other men rescued me from Adak's violent frenzy. I was taken outside, where I lay until I regained consciousness.

After recovering, I told Father Benjamin I would not visit the rehabilitation center again because it was just too dangerous. He smiled and assured me that even though the center could be a hazardous place, it was unlikely that such an incident would happen to me again. He reminded me that the violent patients were always chained and were monitored by the caretakers to protect visitors. Father Benjamin thus convinced me to continue making visits to the rehabilitation center, despite my terrifying initial trip. I needed to share the love of God not only with my family and friends who had been admitted to the center, but also with all the boys and girls who were suffering from mental trauma. I felt it was my responsibility to visit my brothers and sisters and to give them comfort and support during this painful time in their lives.

Apart from the main clinic and rehabilitation center where all refugees could be treated, the Catholic Church also maintained a clinic. The church clinic had been established after Father Benjamin had traveled to Juma to visit the Catholic archbishop for the western region of Ethiopia. He briefed the bishop about the dire conditions in the Pinyundo refugee camp and requested medical assistance. Three weeks later, a group of sisters from Mother Teresa's order were sent by the archbishop to provide needed medical care for the refugees. A truck also arrived with construction workers and materials, and a month later two buildings had been erected: one became the clinic and the other a feeding center.

Those people who were seriously sick, and in need of intensive care were treated at the church hospital. The sisters worked from morning until night caring for hospitalized patients and providing many different types of outpatient treatment. They injected us with quinine for malaria, prescribed medications and cleaned and dressed wounds. In the feeding house, they cooked large quantities of food for patients at the church hospital and those suffering from malnutrition. The sisters also provided care for the mentally ill children admitted to their hospital. Most of the boys whom the sisters treated for mental illness at the church hospital ultimately ended up living in the church compound after their recovery. The sisters treated them like their own sons, and there the boys found happiness and parental love. During this ministry, the churches in the camp not only provided quality medical care, but also spread the word of God among all refugees.

I volunteered to help Father Benjamin and the sisters who were caring for patients, since I was living by that time side by side with them at the church compound. A stronger motivation to work at the clinic was that I felt I had shared the suffering of these critically ill children. We had fled Sudan together and suffered on the long journey to Ethiopia. We endured every day under the same difficult conditions at the refugee camp.

I had varied duties at the hospital at the young ages of eleven and twelve. I turned patients lying in bed who were too seriously ill to turn themselves, fed them and called the sisters when the patients needed more help than I could provide. I would also accompany patients who wanted to walk around during the evening hours at the church compound. Sometimes I played with boys recovering from mental illness at the church playground, so that they could relieve their stress and depression.

One day a strange thing happened, when I was playing with some boys who had recently recovered from mental illness. As we were all kicking around the soccer ball, one of the boys, Dominic Athian Dut, quit playing with us and left the area without my knowledge. After I had passed the ball to one of the boys, I looked around to make sure that all the boys were there, but I was not able to see Dominic around us. My heart started to beat really fast and loud and I began to worry. So I asked the boys to stop playing and help me find Dominic.

I started to run toward the patients' rooms while I was calling his name, and somewhere between the playground and our living area, I found his T-shirt on the ground. I realized that he had become sick again and my distress level increased. I went to his bed and Dominic was not there. I came out of the house and ran toward the chapel.

I saw a crowd of people including sisters and Father Benjamin, standing around the one big tall tree near the chapel. When I went closer, I saw Father Benjamin looking up at the tree and talking to somebody. I knew that was Dominic and I saw him swinging around on a frighteningly thin branch at the very top of the tree. He was threatening to commit suicide by throwing himself down from the top of the tree.

The priest asked why he was choosing death over life; Dominic said that he was tired of a life that was full of suffering and no happiness. Father Benjamin told him that life was precious and could not be replaced when it was taken away, but Dominic refused to come down.

If any one of us climbed up the tree to bring Dominic down, he would go further up and want to throw himself down. So Father Benjamin stopped us and told us to be patient and hope for a miracle to happen. We stayed under the tree for about one hour waiting and talking to Dominic to come down, but he was not moving.

After we had tried almost everything that would have persuaded him, I thought of playing with our sock soccer ball within his sight. I played for about a minute and quickly glanced at him. I had eye contact with him, but did not show him that I was actually looking at him. Two minutes later, he called my name and he asked me whether I wanted him to come and play with me. I first pretended that I didn't want to play with anyone because nobody liked me. He told me that he liked me and that was why he wanted to come down and play with me. I invited him to do so. Everyone was quietly watching.

When Dominic reached the ground, everyone clapped and hugged Dominic and me. Father Benjamin thanked God with a short prayer and then Dominic was taken to his room where he was injected with medicine that is used to calm down mental illness. Dominic later recovered and became the number one student in a class of sixty after conquering his stress and depression.

Chapter 15:
Holy Days

As we neared Christmas 1988, Father Benjamin chose Peter Kuot and me to serve the good Lord as altar boys, a new experience for both of us. I was excited and joyful to be so called by my Lord Jesus Christ. Samuel Lueth and Karlo Kamic trained us to set up the altar, process into the church with the priest, ring the bell and generally assist Father Benjamin during mass. Attired in a white gown, I was nervous during my first mass, but gained confidence as the service continued.

Preparations for the birth of the baby Jesus included clearing debris and weeds around church compounds of all denominations, choir practice and marching band rehearsals. I continued as a singer, but my altar boy duties prevented me from joining the band.

Parades began on December twenty two. Seeing bands from various churches participate and celebrate was a new and exciting experience. Back home, the church groups were limited to Roman Catholic, Islamic and traditional African groups and only the Catholic Church sponsored a band. But now I saw various groups continue to parade through the evening of the 24th.

After dinner on Christmas Eve, we returned to the church to await Christ's birth. Finally, about 11:40 PM, we were directed to our seats. Joyful singing rang throughout the assembly at midnight. That Christmas night was very emotional for me because my spirit was really touched by the Savior's birth. The readings and the music quenched the thirst in my heart and mind. I felt God's mercy and marveled in the lowly birth of a Redeemer who came to this world not only for rich, happy property owners, but also for those who were suffering, homeless and poor.

After welcoming the new year of 1989, we soon moved onto the Lenten season. We fasted during the day on Fridays and only consumed non-meat foods in the evenings. Of course, fasting was not an issue as we had so often known hunger. Following Friday dinner, we prayed the rosary or went through the Stations of the Cross.

Shortly before Easter, Mother Teresa sent videotape about the crucifixion to the sisters assisting the lost boys and girls. Watching this tape, my heart broke and I openly cried at the sight of Christ's suffering. It also reminded me of the deaths of so many of my people in Grandmother's village and beyond. Yet, I was encouraged by Christ to put aside my fear of death and stay strong in my faith.

In the years to come, some holy days would pass almost unnoticed due to being on the run or because our enemies chose those times for renewed attacks. But the memories, although sometimes bittersweet, inspired me to have faith that our Lord would be with me each step of my journey.

Chapter 16:
Arming the Lost

After we had lived in Ethiopia for about two and a half years, all of us started to grow. Many of us were not comfortable with the life we had at the camp and wanted to go back to our homeland. In 1989, before we marked the three-year anniversary, about the half of the children living at Pinyundo refugee camp were taken to a military training base.

This step was taken because many lost boys were escaping from the camp and joining the Sudan People Liberation Army (SPLA). Upon graduation from training, they were heading back to Sudan to defend their wives, children, livestock and land that had been destroyed by the Khartoum government in north Sudan. So when the leader of the SPLA, Dr. John Garang, realized the lost boys' plans, he decided to devise a way to discourage the practice as it was unsafe. Dr. Garang advised Pieng Deng that untrained and unarmed boys' returning to southern Sudan was dangerous. Dr. Garang wanted all the boys to be trained first and then he would provide us with guns so that we would have a fighting chance back home.

This plan settled the boys down. In about a month, our caretakers were called for an urgent meeting in which the caretakers were asked by the camp leader to go back to their houses and pack their belongings. Out of the blue, our caretakers went to the military training camp two and half hours away, leaving us, once again, with no one to take care of us.

Everyone was upset, as our caretakers were the closest things to parents that we had. We had thought that we would all go together, but we didn't know that real military training would be too difficult for us to survive. Our caretakers were taken first because they were going to receive more strenuous training than we would.

This also meant that school was closed, so we just played soccer, volleyball and basket game. Sometimes we swam in the river. After about one month, half of us were taken to the training camp. I was not among the boys who qualified for the first round of the training session. But since my brother Acien was among those who were leaving, I was not happy that I was not on the list to go to Marekas Tadirip. Marekas Tiderip is an Arabic word that means training camp or military training base. So Acien and I agreed that we would pack our clothes together and I would escape and hide along the road. I would join Acien when I saw him on the line. Then, as now, he is a very cooperative and understanding person. He was always ready to help me out whenever I was in a bad situation.

While we were walking toward Marekas Tiderip, I told myself that I was wasting my time for going to the military training camp because my name was not on the roster. But something kept telling me not to quit because I didn't know what would happen. I moved on with courage that God would enable me to succeed despite the trouble I was visualizing ahead.

After two and half hours of non-stop walking, we reached the roadblock of the training camp where we found about five groups of Talimgy, Arabic for military trainer. Surprisingly, these Talimgy were not using the registration list. Instead, each of us were separated from the line and was sent one by one in different directions until five battalions of lost boys were formed. Each battalion was organized into many subgroups, such as companies, platoons and squads.

This process introduced us to the tough nature of the training. We were constantly jogging in line while waiting to be directed to battalions. Then we had to run at full speed towards our groups. If someone chose to walk, he got a horrible and unforgettable punishment, such as being beaten, ordered to roll around on the ground or standing still on one leg. The organization took three to four hours and I was relieved when the exhausting ordeal was over. Best of all, I was placed in the same group as Acien.

We then went to our housing, but the dwellings were too small for the platoons of fifty assigned to each. We overcame that by putting all our bags in the house and sleeping outside. My brother and I spread our sleeping blanket close to the house so that if it started raining, we would be the first people to jump into the small house. We lay down on our blanket and after two hours of rest, we were called to dinner. Before we could even spend two minutes eating, the trainer blew the whistle and we had to leave the food and run toward the assembly area. Those who were not able to run fast because of being hungry and tired were severely punished.

At the gathering, each battalion was asked by their trainers to sing for entertainment for several hours before going to bed. If a battalion didn't know any songs, every member had to create a song to be performed each day. After an hour of singing, our trainer then told us that we would be having an assembly every night. If anyone failed to show up, he would be punished. We would also be running every day and evening.

At last, we were sent to bed. I thought I was going to sleep really well, but I didn't get the adequate rest I anticipated. That very first night we spent at the training camp, we slept for about one and a half hours when all of a sudden, we were awakened by a very heavy rain and sleet. As it started, my brother and I managed to run into the house first. Everyone followed us in and we all ended up standing around, unable to lie down and sleep in the small space.

Our house was quickly filled up with water. The water level increased rapidly and our efforts to block it were unsuccessful. In fact, the entire camp was flooded. It stopped after three hours and our trainers whistled for a general assembly in order to evaluate the damages. Many had been injured; there were even some fatalities.

The injured were taken to the military clinic for treatment and then sent back to their bases. So I passed my first night at the military camp—with a nightmarish welcome.

Our trainer's whistle woke us up early the next morning for the general assembly. We then ran around the camp for an hour while singing the military song and then we started to learn how to stand at ease and at attention. Morning exercise concluded about 7:00 and all our five battalions were brought together in a very wide, open area for another general assembly.

Major General Paul Ring, who was in charge of the base, told us that such heavy rains was common. He said that every day after morning exercise we would go into a forest called Gok Anyuok in order to gather materials to build additional houses. Gok Anyuok is a Dinka word that means Anyuok Forest. Some of us were ordered to fetch some water and carry it with us because there was no water in the forest, while others were given tools for cutting tresses and grasses.

We left for the forest, about a two-hour hike. When we got there, I had a flashback about the worst thing I went through during my exodus to Ethiopia and feared that this forest would be as dangerous as Roor chuol Akol forest had been.

The forest was so dark, quiet and scary that I felt no human being would feel comfortable there. I told Acien about my mood and he felt the same way. I soon learned that every one of us, including our trainers, was experiencing anxiety.

Our trainer told us to stay close to one another while we were cutting down the trees, then wait for one another to finish cutting, and leave the forest together after everyone had collected his assigned materials, such as long, thin and short poles, grasses and ropes.

Acien and I were among the squad of people that was assigned to take care of thin poles. While we were busy cutting down some thin poles from the trees, several lions attacked us. The lions started to chase us and were trying to eat us, separating and scattering us into the forest. Acien and I ran and climbed up on the tall trees. Some of the boys managed to run to other people. At last, the trainers' shooting scared off the lions.

After an hour, we saw that there were no more lions near us, so we climbed down and started to walk back to the base. Brave Acien had advised me to stay calm and find a good way of fighting the lions instead of panicking if they attacked again. We didn't know where to go. About 6:00 P.M., we knew that we were not going to find the way by ourselves and started to call out for help. Luckily enough, there were some trainers who were left behind in the forest to look for those who were still missing. They fired some shots in the air so that we would know they'd heard us. About ten minutes later, the trainers arrived at our scene and we were finally taken back to the military base.

We arrived about 9:30 pm and our platoon and squad members welcomed us with the tears of joy and offered water and food. Our comrades asked us about some of our friends who were missing but we had no idea, since we'd all run off to escape the lions. In time, it was clear that some were gone for good, whether eaten by lions or other animals or simply helplessly lost in that frightening forest.

The following morning, we were all once again sent back to Gok Anyuok despite the attack. This time it was not life threatening because our trainers were constantly firing bullets.

It took two weeks to gather enough building materials and on our third week at the base, we were able to start the foundation of the houses. Then we joined the long and short poles together, roofing the houses and wove the grasses on the tops on the same day. The next day, we finished the walls of the houses with mud; finally, we had adequate shelters after a long month of nightmares and hard work.

With the construction complete, we began our military training. I was extremely excited about the training because I thought it would be much easier than the previous month. Unfortunately, my thinking was quite the opposite of what I was soon to experience.

The first thing we were trained on was marching ahead, right, left and back turn. When all these four steps were put together and I was asked to move in the direction the trainer ordered, I always found myself going in different directions from the rest of the group because it was hard for me to concentrate. Many other boys had the same problem and we usually got punished. It took me some time repeating the same mistake over and over again, but finally I was able to get my confidence and concentration back.

Next up was hiding and fighting techniques. We learned how a platoon could raid a city while another platoon was covering for them.

After several weeks, we mastered these strategies and moved on to weapons training. During the earlier training, we'd used mock weapons because Dr. Garang knew we were too young to handle the real guns properly. There was also the danger of suicide as many of us were depressed. But we were now deemed ready to learn how to operate the AK-47.

As our squad approached the location of our new class, we saw many new AK-47s lying on plastic sheets; two were leaned on the tree. Those two guns were for the trainers who were going to show to us how to operate them. Our senior trainer told us to line up by the gun's side and asked whether any of us knew how to use such a weapon. No one did. He began to demonstrate how to operate an AK-47, starting with how to hold the gun. We were shown how to charge or cock, disassemble, clean and re-assemble it. The trainer repeated the procedures many times before we were asked to try it on our own. Everything seemed to be easy and fine to me at the time and I was confidently waiting for the order. Although only nine years old, I had no doubt I was going to operate an AK-47 without a problem.

We were given an ok to operate the guns on our own, and I first seemed to be doing fine. I handled it properly, but when I came to cocking the gun, I was stuck. I was not strong enough to pull the charge handle. I kept trying, but eventually, I admitted to our trainers that I was not going to be able to pull the charge handle by myself and asked them to help me. One of the trainers laughed at me, but he then came and helped me charge my AK-47.

I disassembled and cleaned my gun successfully, but as I put it back together, some parts were left over. I told our trainers that my gun was correctly assembled, but some parts were left out. Everyone around me, including the trainers, started to laugh and I thought I was the only one that everyone was laughing at. But, in reality, my comrades were giggling because some of them were having the same difficulty. The trainers helped us and soon the whole battalion was laughing about our story. Many continued to make fun of us the entire time we were at the camp.

Our last phase of training was the shooting of the gun and how the platoon could attack the enemy or defend itself. We assembled in a big open field to learn those skills. Two platoons of our trainers were also available at the scene. One of the platoons was to act as the enemy of the other; the enemy platoon hid in the forest nearby. The second platoon was protecting the imaginary city from the enemy. As the exercise got underway, I was very much scared because of the sound of the heavy machine guns. The entire scene of shooting, smoke and people falling dead reminded me of the attack of my home village.

Within five to seven minutes of fighting, the enemy platoon was able to overcome the defending platoon. After the fight was over, those soldiers who acted as if they were killed by gunfire were able to rise up from the dead and rejoin their platoons. I said to myself, where in the world can a person die and then rise up again from the dead if that person is not the son of God or God himself? I was so doubtful and needed to understand the trick that was behind it. Many other boys had the same question, so I asked our lead trainer about it. He said that both sides were using fake bullets and that the major general would further explain them in our last session. After the demonstration, we were able to do that fighting tactic by ourselves some days and complete our training course.

As we awaited our graduation day, we ran out of food. The little food we had was rationed. We would gather fruit near the riverbank during the daytime and then cook whatever we had that evening. Sometimes, if there was no fruit, we didn't eat at all until evening.

A few days before graduation, my friend Eugenio Awak Ring and I ran out of patience. We decided to escape and go back to the refugee camp, get some food and come back with it because we were starving to death. Despite the fact that we knew very well that leaving the base without good reason was unlawful and could result to serous punishment if one was caught, we managed to escape one morning and went back to the refugee camp for the first time in three months. Our friends welcomed us and we were given enough food to eat and more to take back with us.

As we returned, a giant lion attacked us. We climbed a tree and waited there until the lion gave up and left. When we arrived at the base, we found that all our trainers knew about our absence and our bodies started to shiver as if we were caught in a heavy storm. We knew the price we were going to pay was going to be high.

The lead trainer, accompanied by six boys, came to us as Eugenio Awak Ring and I stood at attention. The trainer ordered the boys to chase us into the river, which was about twenty minutes away, soak us down and then bring us back to him. We started to run toward the river while our pursuers were whipping us; we tried to outrun them. At the river, we were told to dive in the water with our clothes on. Back at the base, we were told to roll on the floor numerous times and then to jump like frogs. When told to stand up, we were too exhausted to do so.

I started to beg our trainer to pardon us and give some time to rest a little bit before he could give us another punishment, but my appeal was not accepted. The trainer directed us to pound a tin of grain into grain flour using a mortar. I told him that, although I respected his decision, I simply didn't have the strength to pound grain. When the trainer heard these words, he became annoyed with me and he ordered the boys to keep whipping me until I accepted the punishment.

After a long time of whipping, one of my best friends, James Yai, who was a little older than me, told the trainer that he was going to carry my cross by pounding the tin of grain for me. The trainer listened to him and the boys were told to stop beating me. James and others took me inside our house where I rested. By the time I'd recovered, James had pounded the whole tin of grain and he presented the flour to the sergeant of our platoon who divided it among the platoon's three squads. I gratefully thanked James and told him I was not able to describe what his help meant to me because I was really overcome with joy and happiness. I promised him that he would be my best brother as well as my best friend for the rest of our lives on earth and also in heaven if we happened to go there.

The punishment reminded me about the two tales my grandmother Arek told me three years before when I had visited her village. I came to understand that when one does not comply with rules, the consequences would be severe. I learned that a true friendship is the one in which friends will stand up and be willing to die for one another. During the hardship, James had shown me exactly what kind of friend my grandmother was referring to.

Within a week, we finally graduated and were sent back to the Pinyundo refugee camp in Ethiopia. As we traveled for two hours, we met the other half of the boys from Pinyundo who were now going away for their military training. We wished them good luck and looked forward to seeing them coming back soon.

After their training, they and the caretakers returned and our school opened once again. We had managed to take our grade one final exam the year before and those who passed were promoted to grade two in early 1990. I had passed and was anxiously awaiting the new school year. I was very motivated to continue working hard and further my education.

Chapter 17:
Haunted by the Past

However, my happiness was short-lived. Right after the end-of-first term exam in grade two, I dreamed one night that I had gone back home to my village in southern Sudan and I found that everyone, except my younger sister Aluel, was gone. I found her sitting near a grave outside our home compound. I ran to her, hugged her and asked where everyone was. She replied that many villagers had been killed and others were taken as slaves. Aluel said we were standing at our mother's grave. I started to cry and asked her to leave the grave and go with me but she refused to leave, saying that our mother would still talk with her in the grave and she provided my mother with water and food.

 I did not believe her, but I went closer to my mom's grave and I started to call her name. Immediately my mother replied, calling my name too. I burst into loud tears and called her to come out of the grave and stay with us. She answered that she did not have the power to do so. Her last words were that Aluel and I should leave the village at once because it was not safe for us. Mom insisted that the consequence of disobeying would be severe. I ignored her warning and tried unsuccessfully to dig her out of the grave. Before giving up, I was seriously shocked by something and jumped back from the grave; this made me wake up. I tried to go back sleep and hopefully reach my sister and my mother again, but I was far from sleep.

 Wide-awake, I tried to tell Acien about the dream, but I found that I had lost my voice because of the loud cry I belted out in my sleep. So I couldn't relate the story for a while. When I could tell Acien, he was very much concerned and started to worry. He suggested that we needed to see if our caretaker could help us understand the dream's meaning. The caretaker said the dream could be a flashback of all the bad things I had undergone in my home village and beyond. A second interpretation indicated that I would witness destruction in the future. He said we shouldn't worry too much, because dreams don't always come true. We went back to our house wishing that this weird dream would not mean anything bad because I had already shed many tears for my lost family and countless good friends in the many nightmares I'd already survived in my short life.

I stayed at the camp for about two weeks without hearing any terrible news after the disturbing dream. Right before our schools opened for the grade two, second term, UNHCR told us that the Ethiopian rebels aided by the Sudanese government had attacked Ethiopia's capital city of Addis Abba. Within that very week, the fighting spread all over the country and the Ethiopian government was overthrown by the rebels before the end of 1990. As a result, our lives were affected because Itang refugee camp in Ethiopia was attacked by the rebels. Many people were killed during the onslaught and those refugees who managed to escape had run to our Pinyundo camp.

Soon, our location was attacked as well. While Ethiopians fired on us with machine guns, Sudanese plants dropped bombs. Many people lost their lives and the rest of us were forced out of Ethiopia once and for all. We were left with nowhere to go but to go back to Sudan, which was still engaged in war. We traveled toward the small Sudanese town of Pachalla, which is located at the Ethiopia border.

Chapter 18:
Back to Sudan

As always, this journey was trouble-filled from the start. There was a deadly, heavy storm as we fled Ethiopia. All the small rivers and streams were overflowing, making it really hard for us to travel quickly. Many people lost their lives to that heavy rain. Some were carried away by water and others died of hunger, since we had little time to pack our food during the attack.

Once again, wild animals preyed on us. Hyenas, elephants, tigers, lions, snakes, crocodiles, and bears proved deadly. Hyenas and lions in particular were constantly on the attack. We traveled for two days and nights without rest because the enemy was still chasing us, before reaching a place called Gilo along the border.

As it turned out, Gilo River was the worst and most dangerous place we had yet encountered and casualties were high. River Gilo, one of the deadly waterways at the border of Ethiopia and Sudan, was flooded. There was one boat that could carry about five people, making it really difficult for our group, estimated at of more than 30,000 based on the camp's population, to cross. We were anxious to leave the river behind us and escape the rebels. It wasn't easy, but we managed to make a line and started to use that one boat, everyone waiting for his or her turns. Can you tell us how the estimated numbers were arrived at?

While each of us was desperately waiting to cross the river, the Ethiopian rebels arrived at the Gilo riverbank and started to open fire on us. Many people were shot dead and fell into the water; others jumped into the river even though they did not know how to swim. Unfortunately, most of the jumpers drowned and were carried away by the water, while crocodiles killed others. Some were shot and killed in the water while they were trying to swim.

During all this confusion and horror, a large group of people [including me] who were not able to jump into the water managed to run along the river bank for about three hours until we reached a place where the mountains narrowed the river. A boy who knew how to swim managed to swim across and tie a very thick and long rope around two big trees on each side of the river. Tired, scared and saddened, we were able to use that rope to cross the river at last.

After traveling in the forest for two days without food, we were blessed to meet a group of good villagers of Pachalla in South Sudan who were hunting for animals. The villagers told us not to be afraid of them in Arabic and that they were going to take us to Pachalla town. In the town, our planned destination, we met our fellow refugees and friends who also had been lucky enough to escape from that unforgettable and deadly attack we had suffered at Gilo.

During our arrival at Pachalla, our friends who had gotten there before us did not welcome us. There was no communication among ourselves because we were demoralized by the Gilo attack. I had tried to talk to some guys who were nearby me, but no one would talk back to me. The person I was talking to was I, advising myself to never give up the fight for my life. I told myself to keep on asking God to help me in every bad situation I encountered in the future and trusted that God would enable me to dodge bad fortune in the days to come just as He had helped my friends and me to dodge the bullets that were raining down on us at Gilo. I was physically at Pachalla, but my state of mind was still present at Gilo where I continued to visualize thousands of my people jumping into the water and all of them disappearing in a minute. All I could see was a spark of light: the heavy artilleries that were dropping on us. I had tried to get over these memories, but it was not easy to wipe those images out of my eyes and mind. I sat in one place for more than two hours, watching the live events that had happened at Gilo, which was two days' travel from the town of Pachalla.

Finally, Acien, who might have noticed that some odd thing was going on with me, came and asked why I was sitting still in one place for so long. At first, I was not able to talk back to him, but he kept encouraging me. After a while, it was as if I regained my consciousness and realized that Acien was talking to me. I told him I was very tired and I didn't feel like working around people or talking to anybody. I did not tell him the real reason because I thought I was sleeping and had dreamed about what had happened to us at Gilo. I did not want to share that bad dream with Acien; it was fearful and weird to tell. But my brother realized on his own that I was having bad memories and he discouraged me from thinking too much about that horrible scene. He went on to say I should not worry too much about my life because I had been in dangerous situations before, but God kept looking after us. He would continue to guide us.

"Yanakan, "I replied, using the Dinka word for Amen.

His wise words helped bring me back to normal, although I continued to dream about the harrowing riverside experience.

Indeed, the incident was on everyone's minds as thousands of our fellow refugees had died in a matter of minutes. Our caretakers conducted a head count and found that our band of seventeen thousand lost boys and girls had been reduced significantly to Twelve thousand. The number of adult refugees also dropped, all as a result of a hateful act on innocent and helpless people. It continued to play in my mind like a movie, which I didn't believe to be true. It was hard either to believe it or to erase the images.

We spent a couple of weeks at Pachalla thinking we would move on with our journey to nowhere sooner or later. But eventually, we were told we were going to stay at Pachalla for some time because it was the rainy season and the roads were flooded. Our caretakers also felt that we were somehow going to be somewhat safe at Pachalla because there were some SPLA soldiers stationed there who we thought would protect us in case of an enemy attack.

Chapter 19:
Suffering at Pachalla

After spending just one week at Pachalla, however, our situation went from bad to worse and the list of bad things happening to us kept growing. We were in tents, but as time went by, they were inadequate so we built temporary shelters.

One morning I was sitting on the riverbank when I heard an airplane. Before I could figure out where the sound was coming from, the plane started to release many thousands of tons of bombs. Surprisingly, none of those bombs exploded because the land was all covered by water and mud. So the bombs that had landed on the water and on mud had sunk into the mud and did not blow up. By the grace of God, those falling on dry land didn't explode either. No one could understand this, but I suggested that maybe God was really tired of helpless and innocent children being killed every day for years on end. God, perhaps, had decided not to let any one of us get killed the first day the warplane Antonov bombed us.

After it had released multiple bombs, the plane did not leave us alone. It kept flying overhead. Even though we were very sick and tired of lying down on the stagnant water, we thanked God and felt blessed and lucky. It departed at nightfall, but continued to terrorize us in the days to come.

At the same time, many of us started to die from starvation. There was no food at all to eat at Pachalla. During our first month, all we consumed was the wild fruits of a tree called waak in Dinka. Waak is a type of tree that grows naturally near water. It bears many fruits during the rainy season and loses all its fruit when there is no more rain. But it was not easy for us to go to the forest to gather waak fruits because even the forest was flooded. Despite the great risk, starvation was still forcing us to brave the water in the quest for food. Consequently, many of us drowned and crocodiles and alligators that were living in the floodwater killed others, while more were lost within the depths of the woods.

Starvation wasn't the only health issue threatening our group. Pachalla was exactly like the other places we had lived. Malaria, diarrhea, dysentery, typhoid, tuberculosis and cholera took many lives. In addition to unsanitary conditions, mosquitoes and lack of medicine, the weather was very cold due to frequent rains. As a veteran of worse situations, I thought that my body had adapted and that I was going to resist any disease. My assumption did not come true.

I was the first in my group to register my name in diarrhea's book. One day as I had just finished eating waak fruits and had drunk some water from the river, I soon felt as if my stomach was burning up. I tried to sit down but that did not work out. It felt as if something was cutting my intestines with a razor blade. I tried to lie down on the ground instead of sitting, but the level of pain kept increasing. As it got worse and worse, I started to throw myself down really hard on the ground and roll myself around 360 degrees and then stand up and jump around and throw myself down again. I was crying really badly and I looked as if I were dying. Many people from my group including Acien had gathered around me and they were to trying to calm me down. I couldn't listen through the pain and continued to roll around in agony.

A traditional medicine man from the group immediately went into the jungle and came back a few minutes later with the roots of an unknown tree. He ordered me to chew the roots and then swallow the water of the root. The bitter water was hard to swallow at first. The roots eased the pain level for a while, but the severe stabs soon returned. The pain in my stomach went on and on for several hours until I felt the need to use the restroom. I spent an hour in the restroom, which was actually the forest and certainly had none of the niceties much of the world is accustomed. Then I lay down again on the floor because the ache was still severe. Going to the restroom became my main occupation for weeks to come.

During the first week, I was in too much pain to rest; Acien and our friends lay awake with me. Since waak fruit was the only available food, I ate nothing for two days. I was not going to risk becoming even sicker.

On the third day, Acien, who always took on my burdens, decided to take his clothes to a nearby village to exchange them for some maize grains. Other boys seeking food joined him. He was able to trade his one shirt and one t-shirt for two kilograms of maize. He hurried back to cook the maize. It was through Acien that I had survived that third day. If he had not fed me, that would have been my last day of battling diarrhea. I was fully aware that I would die that day if I had no nutrition. My body was dehydrated, was out of energy and I was losing consciousness. The maize lasted a week and a half, but I was still quite ill.

Acien decided to trade for more food but this time, he had to travel to another village, which was about four hours away from Pachalla, because the closer one was out of rations. As Acien and other boys returned, they were ambushed by a group of bandits who shot and killed several of them. My brother was unharmed; he and two boys who were wounded were the only survivors. They ran all the way back to Pachalla.

I was totally shocked when they arrived. They were carrying no clothes or maize; instead, a boy called Deng Mamer was carrying his intestines in his hands. Some of us collapsed, others stared with open mouths and some were crying. Ironically, Deng Mamer was very relaxed and he kept telling us that he was ok and he was not feeling any pain at all. I couldn't believe this because he was bleeding so badly.

One of our caretakers, Mahdi Atak, rushed to the wounded boys. He quickly put back Deng's intestines back inside and bandaged the wound with a piece of cloth. While Mahdi Atak was treating the injuries, every one of us sat there very demoralized and devastated. There was nothing going on but silence, looks of sorrow and agony in our eyes.

Suddenly, I heard the sound of an airplane, which forced all of us to go and hide because we thought that it was Antonov. Miraculously, the plane belonged to the International Committee of the Red Cross (ICRC). ICRC has been trying to find us since we were chased away from Ethiopia. After the plane had landed in a small open area, we realized it wasn't a warplane. The ICRC delegate then toured the area. The wounded boys were flown away and we didn't see them again.

Having witnessed the courage and determination of these seriously wounded boys, I was very much inspired and I regained my confidence that I could fight my own battle. Deng had shown me that no matter how severe the pain, a person can ease that hurt down if he is determined to fight to the end.

From that moment, I had the strength and energy I needed. I started eating wild fruit, including my enemy the waak fruit. Even though I knew it would probably make me sicker, I had no choice. I also began joining others for conversation and even trying to play soccer. Still, I remained so weak that I could barely stand up and a strong wind could have blown me away.

Chapter 20: Bountiful Food

We spent one month and half surviving on that fruit. As the season waned, a most unusual thing happened in the river. Some may see what transpired next as God's miracle, although scientists would insist it was ordinary migration.

River Pachalla, which had never been a home for lots of fish, suddenly was flooded with them. As time went on, different species migrated in succession. The first to rescue us from hunger was the Mudfish. They were so numerous we could see them with our naked eyes. We could scoop them up in our clothing.

After a couple of days of this much-improved menu, I began to recover. I was able to stand confidently and the severe stomachaches started to fade away. Within a couple of weeks, I was fully healed from my brush with death. I was so thankful to God for being alive and thankful to the river and the fish. I was grateful to Acien and all my friends who stood up with me every day.

After one month of surviving on fish, the ICRC plane again landed at Pachalla. On board were people who would construct an airport to facilitate food deliveries. Hearing that good news raised our morale very high. We immediately started to help with the construction by cutting down trees and clearing stones and grasses. Within two weeks, the landing strip was ready. The next week, a drop of beans and maize was attempted. Tragically, the load landed in a crowd of people, killing many of them.

After the pilot was briefed on the layout of our camp, a successful drop was made, although some sacks landed in mud and water. When the pilot hit the target for the first time, he continued to drop bag after bag. For the first time since we were forced out of Ethiopia, there was plenty of food for everyone.

The dropping of food went on on the following days, along with clothing, blankets, medicines, and mosquito nets. In addition to contributions from the ICRC, people worldwide, especially Americans, sent supplies after seeing our story on CNN television news.

One of these was Manut Bol, the former National Basketball Association (NBA) player. Mr. Bol had seen the starvation and death as covered by CNN. He decided to leave his career and visit us at Pachalla. After he witnessed our suffering, he started to cry because his heart was broken by the pain we were going through. He then donated a huge amount of money to ICRC, which allowed the organization to send even more supplies.

These blessings helped me recover quickly from almost-deadly diarrhea and greatly improved the daily lives of my fellow lost boys and girls. At last, I was able to join my friends in activities such as playing soccer barefoot in the muddy open ground and singing in the church choir.

Worshipping and praying to God was the number one and the most important thing we did. Believe it or not, God was the answer to all the suffering we were going through. Without God, all of us would have been dead by now. It was through our prayers to God and the way that we loved God that carried us during the bad days and the good. He was our source of comfort, strength and encouragement. I knew that God had a plan for me and the rest of those who were suffering with me and that He would one day show me what He wanted me to do for Him. Participating in sports was also important to me and, so no matter what, I would always find an open place to play. My passion helped me put my discouraging troubles behind me.

Chapter 21:
Violence Erupts

Thus, the year 1990 became a relatively good time. Toward the year's end as the floodwaters started to dry out, Ethiopian militia, who were helped by the Sudanese government, attacked the town of Pachalla. The Ethiopian militias on the other side of river Pachalla were fighting two platoons of SPLA who were stationed there to guard the town. After about thirty minutes, the SPLA men forced the militia back to Ethiopia. This victory was attributable to better training and weapons. In addition, the Ethiopians had no way to cross the river. Still, many were killed on both sides. The attack cast us back into the fear that had been lifted by the wealth of food and supplies.

Our fear was justified as soon the Khartoum government started to increase the air bombardment. Antonov began bombing us several times a day and even at nighttime. The drying terrain made the bombs more deadly than before; many casualties were suffered.

This continued for two months, but we maintained the hope that we could move on. Instead, the joint forces of the Sudanese and Ethiopians moved a large number of troops and weapons into the area. Just as the land dried out enough for us to travel, early in 1991, the forces struck. This second attack was almost equal to the one at Gilo, but this time we were on the safe side of the river. With water between our enemies and us, we were able to run away. As we escaped, the town was blasted with artillery shells and gunfire, setting it ablaze.

Acien and I were almost caught because we were close to the path leading into the town and the battle itself. But SPLA soldiers who were exchanging their shots with the enemy before they were chased away from Pachalla by Sudanese government troops distracted the enemies. Additional troops were slowed by the challenges of crossing the river, so we were fortunate to slip away.

Many people were shot dead as everyone tried to run away. As we sped away, a huge rocket landed right in front of us killing all the people who were a little ahead of us. My brother and I threw ourselves on the ground until the smoke dissipated and I began running back in the enemy's direction. I was completely confused and did not recall what direction we were heading in before.

Acien chased me for couple of minutes and right before he could get hold of me, an unknown object hit my forehead, knocking me down. I lay unconscious for some seconds and then I began to cry out loudly that I had been shot, but nobody would stop running and come to see what was going on with me. I kept crying until Acien returned and examined me for wounds.

After my brother gave me a quick check up while dodging the bullets, he told me that I was not shot or injured in any way. He quickly raised me up by my arm and told me to run with him back in the opposite direction from the enemy. He kept urging me to run as fast as I could because the attackers were getting very close to us. We could see them shooting and others were chanting in Arabic, "Hamsik, Hamsik, "which means catch. Other attackers were asking their comrades to stop firing at us because we were children, but they continued chasing us and were laughing at us, too.

I assumed the reason some were laughing at us was because we were running fast and desperately like wounded animals. Acien encouraged me to remain determined and keep running. Many lost boys and girls were shot and killed, but, at last, the sounds of gunfire faded away; we had escaped.

We traveled many hours through the day and night until we reached a small town called Koorchum/ Pakok. There at Pakok, we met a group of the lost that had lived at Jabel Mara. They were attacked at the same time as we were. Naturally, we merged our groups.

We spent one day at Pakok. On the following evening, we heard rumors that the enemy was still following us and could attack the town at any time, so we left at once.

Chapter 22: On the Road Once Again

We traveled toward the southwest of the Eastern Equatorial Region in southern Sudan, heading in the opposite direction of the troops. We had walked and walked for several hours and then the journey started to get tougher as we reached the mountainous region late in the day. The weather began to change, with a cool rain coming in. We experienced deep and dark valleys like nothing we had encountered previously. We had eaten nothing in the three days since the attack.

The firm terrain was difficult to climb up, but coming down also was hard because we couldn't control our speed. Most of us were already injured and many others fell in the deep valley. Once again, we were subject to wild animal attacks. Still, we pressed on for days until we reached a small town called Buma, which means a town in the middle of the mountains.

We rested for some hours at Buma and resumed our journey. We travelled throughout the day and night and on the next morning we reached the border of the mountainous region and the Sarah Desert of Northern Eastern Equatorial in southern Sudan. Dry and hot air welcomed us into the desert. As we journeyed on, the sun's rays became extremely hot as if it had moved down one thousand miles closer to the earth. The sand burned our feet because we wore no shoes. We sweated as if we were competing in a cross-country marathon. We drank the small amount of water we had very quickly and as a result, many of us passed out because of thirst and dehydration.

At this point, our condition was at the red alarm level and each of us was walking silently while waiting for her/his turn to pass out or die. I was praying to God to help us as He had done throughout our exodus and I believe that others were praying to their God, too. Sometime later, good God indeed answered our prayers.

We met a truck convoy in the middle of nowhere. ICRC and UNHCR, who had been monitoring the direction since we were attacked at Pachalla, sent these rescuers. Each beautiful vehicle was loaded with water.

After we had drank enough water, the truck drivers told us that they would carry us to a place called Niarus where the relief organizations wanted us to stay until UNHCR could find a safe place for us. The truck drivers then put about 60 people in each, which had no passenger seats. There were not enough vehicles to transport the entire group; the unlucky ones were left in the Desert. Mostly older children were left behind, including Acien.

As the truck started to move, we all started to fall down on one another because the rough, dusty road made it shake. Soon, we were buried in dust as well. At once, many became car sick as they'd never ridden in a vehicle.

I anticipated these difficulties because I had experienced the same situation when I traveled from Pinyudo to Itang refugee camp for soccer competition. So I had prepared myself mentally and emotionally to accept the ordeal. Those who were not throwing up started to macro-manage those who were by telling them to hold whatever they throw up in their mouth until we reached Niarus. Others said to swallow their vomit. I spoke up and asked everyone to leave those who were sick alone and wait quietly for their turn. A few minutes later, everyone in our truck started to throw up, ending the discussion for good. Thus went the next several hours as we passed through the town of Kapoeta until we finally arrived at our destination close to the Sudanese border with Kenya.

The rest of the boys and girls who did not get transportation had to walk for some days. When they reached the town of Kapoeta that was located between Sarah and Niarus, the Russian warplane Antonov as well as many other jet fighters started to bomb the helpless and innocent young people. They were split into many groups. Many of them ran toward

Niarus, while others, including Acien, ran in different directions. Those heading toward Niarus had to travel for several days before reaching their destination.

Meanwhile, Acien and his group wandered on their own from Kapoeta in southern Sudan all the way to Uganda. There he encountered a Kenyan man and explained his situation. The man smuggled my brother to Nairobi, Kenya, where Acien met other Sudanese refugees. They welcomed him with open hearts to stay with them until he was able to find himself a place to live.

I was very much nervous and concerned when Acien did not arrive with the wandering group. So I started asking people about him. A boy assured me that my brother was not killed and he believed he was doing fine. Although I was relieved, I continued to worry about him. I then prayed to God to help him and all the others in his situation and asked the good Lord to keep him safe until the day we would meet again.

Chapter 23: On to Kenya

Now, it took me some time to adjust to the poor conditions I faced at Nairus. I had to accept the fact that I was going to have to survive on my own without my inspiring leader, my devoted brother. After several months in Nairus, the ICRC and UNHCR learned that Kapoeta, which was some 100 miles away, had been captured from the SPLA by the Sudanese government. We were evacuated into the Kenyan town of Lokichokio, which was at the border of Kenya and Sudan.

Living in Lokichokio was hard because it is located at the edge of the desert in the Turkana district. Thus, Lokichokio is very humid, dry and hot. There is little drinking water and our food supply started to shrink. Worse, it was an insecure area. Some locals could come and attack us at night and take away all our food. Cattle rustling were common.

Despite all these problems, we had stayed at Lokichokio from the beginning of 1992 until August of that year. When UNHCR learned that the Sudanese government was going to bomb the town, we were taken into the middle of the Turkana District to Kakuma.

The journey from Lokichokio to Kakuma was unique from all the journeys we have been through over the past five years. UNHCR did not allow any one of us to walk on foot because of frequent ambushes by bandits. So we traveled by truck with police protection. In addition, the high heat would have made walking dangerous.

With insufficient trucks, we moved in groups based on our living zones. I was very happy when I finally left Lokichokio because the short journey was not bad compared to our trip from Sarah desert to Nairus. I was hoping for a better life since the Sudanese could not pursue us into Kenya.

We were welcomed at our new home by a dust storm, which made it difficult for us to see clearly. Of course, the truck drivers had the same problem, so they had to use headlights in order to see, even though it was daytime. The semi-arid, treeless region was prone to such storms. When a dry wind blew, it caused storms that could last for weeks or even months.

As it had not rained in years, the locals were closer to starvation than we were because we were able to receive some food from UNHCR. The good future and better life I was hoping to find at Kakuma was far beyond the reality. All I had seen the first day showed me the true colors of what life there was going to be.

We were settled in a wilderness about a half hour away from Kakuma. UNHCR supplied us with drinking water, food, clothing and material for building our shelters. It took some time before we finally began to sleep in the shelters. Then, our caretakers decided to begin our education once again.

The caretakers started immediately to train us under what few trees there were. UNHCR later was able to build schools for us, but our learning at the refugee camp was not very effective because of the many problems at Kakuma.

Kakuma was humid and extremely hot throughout the year with temperatures up to 120 degrees during the day. This made studying in classrooms without air conditioning difficult. Many of us would start to complain from headaches and neck pain. Some even died from these heat-related illnesses. I myself had suffered many times, but God blessed me and helped me to recover from the heat exposure. However, as many were dying everyday from the heat, our teachers decided that we should go to school in the morning only. Although this did not eliminate the problem completely, it did help.

Many diseases such as malaria, diarrhea, typhoid, anemia, cholera and HIV/AIDS were rampant, killing or disabling my comrades. I was fortunate to recover from bouts with two illnesses.

Our food supply was cut and had to go further because UNHCR was still bringing many refugees from several African countries due to war. In fact, Kakuma refugee camp came to be one of the largest such places worldwide.

We received our food from UNHCR every two weeks. Each one of us was given a ratio of two kilograms of maize grain, one kilogram of wheat flour, one cup of cooking oil, one kilogram of beans and a few teaspoons of salt. We tried to cook this food separately, but could not even stretch it to last a week. Then we tried working in groups of five, pooling our rations. Even still, the supplies didn't allow five people to have two meals daily.

So we dropped down to one meal most days. Then the rations lasted about 12 days, much closer to the next delivery date. However, the three days that we spent without food were very challenging and came to be known as black days. "Black" referred to the lack of fire in our kitchen for that time.

To get by, we would go to school early in the morning and spend the hot afternoon gathered under one tree. We would make jokes about the previous fasts and struggles we had been through and poke fun at each other for our reactions to those situations. We laughed and sang until evening came. Then we would spread our sleeping material outside in an open area near our houses, again gathered as one group. We would tell stories until we fell asleep.

Insecurity threatened us at Kakuma. The local people were starving, so we shared our food with those who came by. But the bad guys were not satisfied with our help and would come back at night and shoot at us. Although they killed many of our fellow refugees, this was also a diversionary tactic so accomplices could steal our food and clothes. Eventually, UNHCR hired some local police to guard us during the night, but they were ineffective in protecting us. So we worked with kind villagers to look after ourselves. We swapped half of our food for branches of thorn trees, which we used to build fences. This barrier, along with our own lookout details, helped curb the criminal activity.

We still had our enemies, however. The Sudanese government continued to be a very big threat. In 1993, Sudanese authorities smuggled some collaborating politicians from southern Sudan into the Kakuma camp. They were sent there to create more trouble among the southern groups. They divided us by bribing their tribe members with money to mobilize against other tribes. This led to serious fighting, including deaths, between the Nuer and Dinka tribes. Finally, UNHCR settled the Nuer tribe 30 minutes away from the Dinkas, but that did not bring an end to all tribal fighting.

Even though our lives were like those of prisoners on death row waiting for execution day, we did not lose our hope of struggling to survive for a better tomorrow in the wilderness. To keep our dreams alive, we engaged in positive activities, such as religious worship and sports that promised hope and light during the dark and pointed the way to a better future.

The Kakuma refugee camp was comprised of various nationalities of diverse faiths. Worship was available for each group. Islam and Christianity were the most common and as in previous camps, established worship centers. In my chapel where I used to pray, there were many other activities such as Bible study and choir. I was a member of both a small Christian community, which offered programming, and a choir member. Some years later, I became a choirmaster there in my refugee camp church.

Both Bible study and singing in the church were very inspiring and helpful to me because they brought peace to my mind and comfort to my soul whenever I was down. The scripture I was sharing with my fellow brothers and sisters would heal the pain that I was going through and restore my hope for better days. The songs would nourish me, filling me with happiness and joy and would even suppress my hunger.

Due to the long drought, the trees under which we worshipped had few leaves, offering little shade. After a very long time of praying through the hot, dusty days, God sent rain to Kakuma for the first time in almost a decade. The delightful downfall suppressed the dust, increasing leaf production; at last, Kakuma was green and more moderate in temperature. Christian churches started to expand quickly under the lush trees. Later, actual structures were erected. Youth activities, such as choir competitions, sprang up entertaining the entire camp. The church leaders made a connection with fellow Kenyan Christians to sponsor those boys and girls who had finished elementary school successfully.

Church made a real difference in our survival at Kakuma. It was so important, in fact, that we still went to church despite the many shootings that went on during prayers.

Sports again emerged as another important part of our daily lives. After schools were built for us, each school formed teams for boys' and girls' sports, such as basketball, soccer and volleyball. The competition entertained the entire camp and helped relieve stress.

I played for my elementary school's boys' soccer team. After a couple of years, my skills improved and I was selected for the Kakuma refugee soccer central team, which represented 80,000 refugees. Our team represented the camp at district and provincial levels, as well as the national level, if we happened to win at all the preliminary levels.

Chapter 24:
A Return to Competitive Soccer

When the Catholic Church introduced their youth program, which included athletics, I was chosen for the Holy Cross Catholic Church soccer team. This team represented the refugees at the diocesan level within the Turkana district. I was very excited and felt proud of what I had done so far on my own without my parents. This was the second time I had represented the entire refugee camp and I came to deeply understand that hard work would help me to fulfill my dreams. It had been my goal to play for my country's national soccer team one day if it ever became peaceful enough for me to return to Sudan. Sadly, that dream was unlikely to be fulfilled because there was no guarantee that war would ever cease in my homeland.

My first match for the Kakuma refugee central soccer team was against the Turkana District central team. As we started to play, the opponents were winning in the first half by scoring two goals to nothing for our team. In the second half, our team struggled until we brought the game to a two-two tie. Near the end of 90 minutes of play, I was able to score the winning goal! My accomplishment was emotional and heartwarming not only to me but also to all my teammates and even to all our fans, because none of us believed that we were going to win that match. Although Turkana was in better shape, had better equipment and was shutting us out, our team realized that with determination we could finish strongly. We returned to camp with great happiness for once. That day no one was disappointed or discouraged about possible career-ending injuries, a real possibility every time we played.

One of the worst injuries of my playing days occurred a few months later during the Daniel Comboni soccer tournament in 1996. Daniel Comboni was an Italian Catholic missionary who had gone to Sudan to spread the word of God. He later died and was buried there. Since Comboni had dedicated his life to the people of Sudan, he is honored every October 10th. During Daniel Comboni Remembrance Day, the youth group used to organize different sports.

There were more than twenty soccer teams competing in this event. The Holy Cross team won all its games leading up to the finals without any serious injury. In that last decisive game, we faced St. Peter and Paul. We scored two goals during the first half and no players on either side were hurt. The second half was scoreless until the last minutes. One of my teammates passed the ball to me in the air within the six-yard box. I ran toward the ball and tried to kick it in the air when the goalkeeper collided with me in the air as we fought for the same ball. He jumped on me with his feet on my chest and his fist on my mouth, knocking me down very hard. I lay unconscious and perfectly still.

The whole crowd of people ran over and somebody that I did not know resuscitated me. I was now able to breathe, but I was still unconscious. I was then rushed to the hospital where I remained in a coma for more than twelve hours. Slowly, I regained my consciousness and could recognize those around me. But what I did not know what had happened to me and why I was in hospital. I tried to talk, but I was not able to open my mouth because my lower lip and my tongue were cut open and swollen. Broken ribs didn't help matters.

So I remained silent for several weeks. Many lost boys and girls, including Nancy Abur, came and visited me every day and prayed for me, which actually helped me with my recovery process. I then asked what had happened to me and the whole story was explained. William Mou was the one caring for me when I was in hospital. I was released from the hospital and went back to my group. Although I will never forget that horrible injury, I also will never forget the immense love and support I received during that time. I survived the nightmare because of the care of others. I would have died on the spot if the folks at the scene of accident had not helped me.

Moving on with my recovery process, it took me several months to recover about 80 percent and to be able to walk and breathe properly. I decided not to play soccer anymore because I felt that additional injuries could end my life prematurely. But without playing or even watching others practice, I was lonely and bored in the evenings as almost everyone participated in soccer.

Chapter 25: Reconnecting

After a few weeks, I got frustrated with my situation and decided to take a walk every evening to the International Committee of the Red Cross's communication center. This allowed refugees to have a connection with their relatives around the world by sending written letters. Every day, I hoped for a return letter, but came up empty handed for two and a half months.

One evening when I checked on the board, I surprisingly found my name. I double-checked my name to make sure that I was right and then I went inside the office and got my letter from the mailman. Before I could open the letter, I realized that my brother Acien who was separated from us when Antonov attacked us at Kapoeta had sent it! He was living in Nairobi and was doing well. I wrote back to him and told him that I was doing fine and wished to see him soon. I told him that I was going to try really hard to go to Nairobi to see him, so I asked for his address.

After two months, I received Acien's reply telling that he was living in a place called Kibera in Nairobi. Kibera is a slum area with low rents and thus, it is more affordable for poor people like Acien. I wanted to go to him but I did not have money for transportation.

I called on the Catholic pastor Father David Wanyama and asked him if he could help me with ten shillings (Kenyan money) which is less than fifty cents US. I wanted to buy some seeds to cultivate. Pastor Wanyama was very generous, giving me twenty shillings. I immediately went to market and bought some collard green and okra seed.

I prepared a garden near the water tap that was close to my group. I dug a big hole near the tap and made a channel in which to collect waste water for irrigation. After two months of irrigating my garden and taking good care of it, my crops were ready for harvest. The sale of these vegetables financed my trip.

With bus fare in hand, I wrote to Acien for travel advice. He suggested I use a Kenyan bus and he would pick me up at the station. I let him know my departure date, several weeks away, so he would receive the letter in time. I was growing impatient for the reunion with my brother whom I had missed so much.

At last, the appointed date in 1996 arrived and I went to the bus station. As I was buying my ticket, the bus driver asked me whether I had a traveling document from UNHCR; I did not. He insisted that if I did not have that document, it would be hard for me to travel to Nairobi because there were many police roadblocks from Kakuma to Kitaly. I told the driver that these documents were difficult to get and persuaded him to have pity on me and try his level best to get me through the road-blocks. The driver was a very kind person who had a good heart to aid those who are helpless. He broke into tears when I started to tell him the situation I had been through. He agreed to hide me inside the luggage storage area in the bus.

The bus traveled for about nine to ten hours while I struggled for breath in the storage area. When the bus reached Kitaly, the driver bustled over to release me. He let me rest for a while and he then took me to the Kenyan bus station at Kitaly town where I took another bus to Nairobi. I assured him that I would be visiting him upon my return.

I began to feel good and happier in the second bus. There were nice seats and the bus driver was playing church music that made me feel as if there was a choir from heaven singing. There was even food for sale.

Chapter 26: Life in a Big City

The bus arrived at Nairobi after eight to nine hours on the road. As I got out of the bus, I started to panic and got confused because the bus station was located between very tall buildings. I was really very afraid that those buildings might fall down on me at any time. That was my first time in a big city and everything seemed dangerous to me. Conductors who are called makanga in Swahili were making a lot of noise trying to call customers onto their buses. Many people were running in different directions, which made me think that the city was under attack.

As I was waiting for Acien, three different groups of makangas started to fight over me because each wanted me to take to their bus, bound for some unknown destination. One group of makangas grasped my right hand, another group took my left hand and the third group pulled my waist and all three were all pulling me in different directions at the same time. They kept pulling me as I cried until a stranger stopped these makangas and told them he would pull off my arms if they continued. My rescuer then asked me where I was going. After a short conversation, he advised me to be careful and was on his way.

However, two other men approached me right after he left. One said to me in Swahili, "Leta Pesa, " which meant "give me money. " The second man opened his jacket halfway, showed me the pistol that he had hidden in his waist and told me that they were going to kill me if I did not give them money. Without hesitation, I put my hand in my pocket and took out my last 50 Kenyan shillings and gave it to the strangers. They also took my bag and left me with nothing.

At last, Acien and I found each other. We hugged one another and went to the Kibera bus station some blocks away. This was a frightening walk for me. As Acien and I were walking across a very busy road, I was caught up in the middle by a very big truck that was running down the road toward me at the speed of 60 miles per hour. My brother, who was walking ahead of me, thought that I had crossed the road with him. When he looked over his shoulder, he saw the truck bearing down on me. Acien, being accustomed to the heavy traffic, quickly ran back and moved me away. I missed the truck by about two seconds! Once again, I owed my life to my dear brother. We moved on, now walking hand in hand.

Finally, safe in Acien's home, we rested for a while and then he began to cook the little food he had. We feasted on the meager rations, knowing we were leaving nothing for the next day. Although our reunion had been a nightmare, we tried to stay happy and thankful to God that our three years of separation had finally ended.

On the next morning, my brother asked me to walk with him to the Diocese of Rumbek and Lutheran World Food Federation to ask these two Christian organizations for food. We walked for three hours. We asked the security personnel who were guarding the gate at Rumbek Diocese to let us go ask the Bishop for food assistance, but we were denied permission. This was because we did not have legal documents to live in Nairobi. The Diocese restricted aid to those refugees who were permitted to live in the city because of insecurity in the refugee camp. We were met with the same response at the Lutheran World Food Federation.

So, as we returning back home hungry, hopeless and tired, we came across a soccer field where many people were practicing. I asked Acien if we could go and watch for a few minutes. While watching, we realized that those who were practicing were Sudanese, for they could speak Arabic. I began to become interested in playing soccer again despite the fact that I had told myself I would not after recovering from my earlier injuries. But I felt like going back because of the way Coach Al Zihad was training the team.

His style was interesting and inspiring. Al Zihad's demonstration of ball movement and tactics was impressive. So I asked a very hungry Acien to stay until game's end so I could speak with Al Zihad. When practice wrapped up, I immediately approached the coach and introduced myself to him, told him that I was impressed with his coaching ability and would like to join his team. He hesitantly agreed to allow me to train with the team. He also told me that I had approached at the right time because a friendly match with one of the Kenyan teams, Impala Club, was coming up and some of his players were out due to injuries. I promised to see him for that game the very next day. Before I could say farewell to Mr. Al Zihad, he somehow realized that Acien and I were hungry and had nothing to eat. He put his hand in his pocket and gave me money, which he said I should use for bus fare for the match. We could not believe our eyes when we saw the coach giving me money because our daylong efforts to find food had been unsuccessful. We felt that it was a miracle from God. We thanked Mr. Al Zihad profusely for his generosity and we left with a lot of energy and happiness because we could survive another day.

On our way back home, we bought groceries and reserved some money for transportation. After our unexpected meal, I was ready for sleep, although also anxious about the next day's match.

The next morning came and we were able to have breakfast before heading to the soccer field. By the grace of God, I was able to score the first goal. A teammate scored two more to give us the victory. Coach Al Zihad was very excited about my play and he invited Acien and me to his house after the game. On our arrival at his house, his beautiful wife Sarah, his daughters, Aboa and Sandra, and his son Jimmy, warmly welcomed us. The family then served delicious food and cool juice.

The Al Zihad family began to ask us about our family. We told them that our father was shot in the chest during the attack on our village. We told them that we had not heard anything about the rest of our people. After a long pause, they expressed their sympathy. Mr. Al Zihad apologetically told us that he too is a Muslim and he was so sorry about what had been done to our people. This was very irritating to me because I used to hate the name Muslim to death. I held every Muslim accountable for the destruction, suffering and agony that had brought to my people and me; I really did know who was responsible for all these crimes against us. Al Zihad was wise enough to realize through our body language that we weren't feeling so friendly any more. He told us that he was also a victim of those crimes.

Al Zihad told us that he used to be a policeman and one day he was told to kill people during the night, but he refused. He was then thrown in jail and the government ordered some of his colleagues to kill him overnight. Fortunately, one of his best friends who was working with him at the station got him out of jail. Al Zihad and his family then fled Sudan on foot to Egypt and from Egypt to Kenya.

So through Al Zihad, we learned that it was not all Muslims who were killing the people of southern Sudan, but some radical Muslims who were mobilized by the Sudanese government to slaughter the innocent in the name of Islam. Those Muslims who opposed the genocide were also killed. I therefore held back my hate and I began to accept each and every Muslim in my heart as my brother and sister in one God. I left, knowing I could continue with soccer.

After the time I had spent training with Coach Al Zihad, I had gained a lot of playing skill as well as coaching skill. He and the team helped my brother and me by paying our house rent and providing us with food. And most importantly, he was like a father to all of us who were in his team, even though the majority of us were Christians. Because of Coach Al Zihad's generosity, I was able to stay with Acien in Nairobi for two and a half months without worry. But, when my return to the camp was two weeks away, I started to worry about my brother's future because once I left Nairobi and the soccer team that assistance was likely to dry up. On the other hand, I maintained faith in God and was hoping that He would help Acien.

Miraculously, a Catholic nun, Sister Luis, granted my brother a scholarship within a week of my departure. The scholarship was going to cover his tuition for electrical training for two years and another year to work for the school under the sister's sponsorship. He would receive pocket money that would cover his rent, food and school equipment. Sister Luis sent a letter to the UNCHR headquarters in Nairobi and got him a protection letter. This document was provided to my brother as a student in order for him to stay in Nairobi without police harassment. When this miracle happened, we were overcome by happiness and we both started to cry. We had not expected such a blessing because Acien had tried really hard for many years to find a scholarship. I could leave Nairobi without worrying about my brother because his being patient all this time had paid off.

Chapter 27: A Return to Kakuma

My journey back to Kakuma was better than going to Nairobi because I did not need to hide in the luggage storage area on this bus ride anymore. While the police were keen to prevent refugees entry to the city, they had no qualms about their departing.

After resting a couple of weeks back at camp, I decided that I should pass on the knowledge and inspiration that I had acquired from Coach Al Zihad. So I went to different groups and selected about 26 soccer players who represented diverse backgrounds, religions, and nationalities. I named the team Black Eagle. I was the head coach and William Mou became my assistant. At the age of 16, in 1996, I was coaching for the first time. Some players were my own age or older.

In 1998, Black Eagle became the best team among more than 20 teams at Kakuma refugee camp and almost 95 percent of the population became a Black Eagle supporter. Black Eagle could play a quality soccer game, was a mixture of the various nationalities in the camp and most importantly, the team was a symbol of peace, love, unity, and inspiration to all. Regardless of religious or other differences, everyone would come together and support my blended team. I was thrilled that Black Eagle could inspire the camp just as Coach Al Zihad had encouraged me. That achievement kept me moving on and on whenever my morale was down.

Having said that, there was a major setback to the progress of the team that same year. At that time, we had spent six years in the camp and the situation got worse and worse. There was a shortage of food, local people shot refugees every night and many were dying daily from diseases. Many Lost Boys and Girls, including some of my players and friends, decided to go back to Ngatinga in southern Sudan to search for food and security.

One month later, I was told that one of my best friends, Mathet had stepped on a land mine and lost one of his legs as a result. I was told that he was admitted to Lokichokio Hospital at the border of Kenya and Sudan and nobody was taking care of him. So William Mou and I went there to take care of him.

Chapter 28:
Real Hope at Last

While I was at Lokichokio, the U.S. Catholic Conference of Bishops finally communicated our long-term suffering to the United States government. The Americans decided to resettle all the lost boys and girls of Sudan in their country. The U.S. sent a team to prepare everyone to immigrate in 1998, 11 years after I first fled my home village. Everyone was registered and photographed. When my turn came, my group mates knew that I was still in Lokichokio, so one of them, Mel Deng, pretended to be me. His picture was taken and then stuck in my file as me. When I returned, he told me and I thanked him for helping me out and waited to see what would happen in the next step.

As preparations were underway, terrorists attacked American embassies in Nairobi, Kenya and Darussalam, Tanzania. That brought a halt to our preparation. We were especially distressed because the attackers were followers of the same Osama Bin Laden who had contributed to the killing in Sudan. I was angry enough to kill these terrorists myself. We had waited and waited for our resettlement program to resume soon, but it did not happen that year. 1999 came and went without the resettlement program reopening. Finally in 2000, the resettlement team returned and started to interview us. When my turn came, I ended up being in hot water because the photo clearly was not me. The lawyer asked me what had happened and I explained the situation. He refused to conduct the interview and asked me to bring some documents that would prove my identity.

Because of the confusion, many lost boys and girls were interviewed after me and resettled, while I was still waiting to be rescheduled for the second interview. I was finally interviewed in 2001, documentation in hand. After I passed the screening, I was then put on the waiting list. Acien also was accepted and awaited his new life in America. In addition, some of the lost boys and girls who were my best friends, including Nancy Abur, started to leave the refugee camp to travel to America, leaving me at Kakuma with no connection with them. The departure of my friends had seriously affected me and others left behind because we felt that we were never going to meet again.

While I anticipated my resettlement, Bin Laden orchestrated the September 11 attacks in the United States. This was very devastating to me because of the many people who lost their lives. It also meant another wait for those of us who were eager to depart. I was alarmed because I had been running away from violent attacks in Africa and thought that United States was the only place that would be safe. When I heard that Bin Laden had attacked the U.S, I lost the hope of finding a place where I could stay without worry about insecurity.

I stayed at the refugee camp for other two years without hearing anything about my departure to America. Then in 2003, my brother was finally flown to America, leaving me alone in Africa. After a couple of months, he started to send me money every month. This solved my hunger problem.

However, I was still facing attacks from the locals and the threat of disease. 2003 passed and nothing came up for me regarding my coming to America. I became very frustrated and ran out of patience because many who had finished the process with me had left more than two years previously. I was still living at the Kakuma refugee camp where there was no hope and future at all.

One week later, in the very beginning of 2004, a few months before I turned 24 years old, my name and the names of others who had been waiting with me all this time finally appeared on the public bulletin board at the camp for departure to America. When I saw my name, I became confused and shocked because it seemed to me as if I was dreaming. I did not believe my eyes. After waiting and hoping for so many years, we were given a mere three days to prepare before our departure.

Chapter 29:
Coming to America

When the appointed day arrived, we were taken to a local airstrip where a small plane would take us to Nairobi, then a big plane to America. After we boarded, the flight attendant came and tied a seatbelt on each of us. When the plane took off, I was very afraid because I had never flown before. I felt like my stomach was falling down inside me as the plane went higher and higher into the sky and became unstable. I was ready to cry out to the flight attendant for help when the plane gained stability. It took us two hours to arrive at Juma Kenyatta International Airport in Nairobi and during the landing; I felt the same way as when the plane was taking off. But this time, I tried to control my fear and my feelings because I had figured out that I was not going to die.

We were then taken to a reception center in Nairobi called Gold where we spent one week before our departure to America. We then were told where our final destination would be. We were given an orientation about western culture at the time. My roommate-to-be was Peter Piol and we were told that we were to be resettled in Las Vegas, Nevada. That was good because Las Vegas was said to have warm weather like the weather we were used to. We were very happy about that.

On February 1, we were taken back to the airport where we finally said good-bye to Africa and left Nairobi at 10:00 p.m. for America. I was so emotional that I had no concerns about the flight itself. All I wanted was to get out of Africa and try living somewhere else, regardless of where that might be.

After awhile, the flight attendant started to serve food and drink, but I would not ask for any because I thought that I was going to be charged and I had no money. Some hours later, one Good Samaritan flight attendant came to me and asked why I did not ask for anything. He then told me that the food and drink were included in my ticket and I did not need to pay. He went to the kitchen and came back with a variety of food and drinks. All the food he brought to me was western food and none of the aromas appealed to me except the sandwiches. I asked him to give me one sandwich and orange juice and was relieved to learn that this was one part of my journey that would not involve hunger.

We traveled for about eight hours and landed in Brussels in Belgium. After a two-hour layover, we headed for New Jersey. I was sitting in a window seat on this flight. When the plane was about to land, I felt very cool and started to shiver. I then decided to look out the window to catch a glimpse of my new country. To my despair, the land was covered with snow! When the plane landed, it was colder still.

We went inside the airport thinking that Newark was our final destination, but Peter and I were told that we had more travel ahead. We had to wait again for several hours before we could leave for Las Vegas. The non-stop flight finally got us to Vegas around midnight.

Chapter 30: Welcome to Las Vegas

As we were walking down the hallway in the airport, we met with our caseworker, Taban Dogu, who received us very warmly. We followed him to his van so that he could drive us to the house that he had rented for us. While we were walking to the parking lot, I encountered one of the challenges I was going to deal with in my new homeland. I became very cool, even in the supposedly warm desert city. I told Taban and he started to laugh at me and told me that the weather in Las Vegas was not that cold compared to other cities in the United States. He assured me the long, chilly walk would be rewarded with a heated van ride.

Taban picked up McDonalds hamburgers and French fries on the way home. Taban took us around the house and showed us our bedrooms, bathroom and how to use the toilet. He demonstrated using the stove and the heat. I did not understand all the instructions immediately. I asked Taban to repeat everything he had taught and took notes. I knew that we were going to have to operate everything in the house by ourselves and if we did not follow Taban's directions properly, we might mess up everything.

Peter and I tried to eat the fast food, but we could not because we found the smell very strange. So, we slept without eating during the first night in America. On the following morning, Peter woke up very hungry. He went to the kitchen and turned the stove on high and then started to cook some food while I continued to sleep. While his stew was cooking, he decided to go and sit down for a while. He forgot that he was cooking and the stew caught fire; smoke billowed throughout the house. A couple of seconds later, a smoke detector went off in the living room with a very loud noise that woke me.

I quickly rushed to the living room and found Peter confused about what to do in the middle of the mess he had caused. He did not know how to turn off the smoke alarm, and I too was confused and had forgotten how to turn it off. So I turned off the stove first because the flames shot up high and I was afraid that the house was going to catch on fire. I opened the door for ventilation and then took out my notebook. At last, I figured out how to silence the screaming alarm. Each of us sat down alone in his own corner without talking to one another.

When the smoke cleared, we went back to the kitchen and did some clean up and then started to cook another meal. This time, I stayed in the kitchen while the food cooked. I dished up plates for both of us. I started to eat, but Peter could not because he was affected by the incident. So he spent his first two days in the land of plenty without taking a bite. He regained his appetite on the third day, after learning healthy respect for American kitchens.

We had spent three days without any one visiting us because many of the lost boys who were living in Las Vegas worked the night shift in casinos and slept during the day. Although they were anxious to meet us, they had to wait for their days off. Taban did come on day three and drove us to a social service office where we applied for food stamps.

Taban burst out laughing when Peter told him about the cooking disaster. He thanked God that nothing bad had happened and he told Peter not to worry about it because the same mistake had been committed by many of the lost boys. Taban assured Peter that it was only a matter of time before he learned to cook without a problem. We also had the power company put the power in my name and arranged for a telephone.

On the following day, Taban drove us to the school where we registered for English as a Second Language and computer classes. He showed us the bus station we'd use to get around town.

Once the phone was installed, I called my brother Acien who was living in Atlanta and told him that I had finally made it to America. He was so excited about my arrival and welcomed me to America. I called several other fellow lost boys. Our compatriots in Vegas took us around the city and showed us its beauty.

After I had spent one month in America, I realized that it was up to me to make my life successful. So I began to go to English as a Second Language and computer classes every morning while I was waiting to receive my work authorization papers. That process took about four months.

With my permit finally in hand, I went to casinos early each morning to fill out applications for work and attended classes in the evening. My English instructor advised me that since I had completed high school in Africa, I could probably study at a higher level. I took a placement test at Las Vegas Community College and I was placed in English 111 and in Math 93. I was very pleased with this and called Acien to share the news.

After my brother had congratulated me, he told me that he had planned to call me too because he had heard from a lost boy who had gone to Sudan recently. His mother told him that she used to live with my mother at a refugee camp in the northern part of Sudan. I immediately started to cry when Acien told me this because I'd been sure that both of my parents had been killed back in 1987. He added that our mother was seriously ill and suffered from mental illness due to the destruction of our home land, the hard life she had had at the refugee camp and fifteen years with no word from us. Acien assured me that he would try to go to the refugee camp and take her to Kenya or Uganda where she could find treatment. I said I would try really hard to find a job so that I could help him in raising the money.

Chapter 31: Working in America

One week after I had received this news, I got my first job in America at Wal-Mart. I was very excited to have the opportunity to help my mother. I now thought that I would be working and going to college at the same time but it did not happen that way as my schedule at Wal-Mart was not permanent. I worked during the morning hours the first week, and then had to work the second shift the next week and work on the third shift the following week. My unstable schedule made it hard to go to school, but I didn't want to quit work. So what I did was to give up school for some time. Even still, the Wal-Mart job was very challenging to me because it was located an hour and a half away and after taking a bus, I still had a half hour's walk to the store. It was difficult to use a bus when I worked late hours.

One day, I was working in the evening hours and found the bus station closed after work. So I decided to walk all the way home and as I made my way, three people attacked me. They held me down, took my wallet out of my pocket, beat me up really badly and then left me to go home. I went right to bed when I finally got home.

On the following morning, I called my friend Bol Magok and told him about the attack. He advised me to quit that job and keep applying at the casinos that were near my apartment. I told him that I needed that job really badly and I had not even received my first paycheck. He understood and generously bought me a bicycle for transportation.

After a month of biking to work, I received very devastating news from my brother. He told me that my mother and some other refugees had become tired of the suffering at the refugee camp and decided to go back to their villages in southern Sudan after they had learned that a peace treaty had been signed between the rebels and the government of Sudan.

On their way, they had to travel two days through a jungle. They were attacked by a group of lions and my mother was killed. I was devastated and shocked by the news, because for the past two months I'd been overjoyed thinking she was alive. I then called my manager at Wal-Mart and told him that I was going to be absent for several days while I grieved for my mother. My manager told me that it was alright for me to stay home, but that I would lose my job. I did not qualify for vacation or leave of absence as I had worked there only three weeks.

After a week, I went back to work and learned I really had been fired. A month later, I decided to accept the tragedy as a part of my life journey and move on. So I went to Cheyenne Community College for fall classes. I had registered for English 111, computer 101, and math 93. I also decided to earn an American high school diploma. I did the high school work online while attending college classes.

While I was busy with my studies, I was called by the Mirage Hotel and Casino for a job interview. I needed the job and was hired as a utility porter for the night shift. I started work at 12:30 midnight and got off at 8:30 A.M. From there, I went to the bus station to go to school. I would come home, shower, eat and do my high school and college homework before I could go to bed. I was getting three to four hours of sleep each day.

While at the Mirage, I began to like American food because the hotel offered a buffet for employees during their breaks. I fell in love with fried chicken and hamburgers.

After two months, I began to find it difficult to work and go to school at the same time without having my own transportation. So I worked for one more month at the Mirage in order to buy a car with my $2900.00 savings. My friend Abraham Makueeth helped me look for cars. It was tough as I did not yet have credit. Finally, I was then given approval to buy a car because we found a dealership that did not care about the credit. We decided to buy a 1997 Mitsubishi Mirage. Without knowing anything about the car, I just went and did the road test with Abraham. I thought that the car was good and paid $2500.00 as a down payment. The car was $6800.00 and I was going to pay the owner $250.00 every month.

The car was not inspected when it was sold to me, so we first drove to a station. The car failed the inspection so I had to take the car back to the dealer and ask him to repair it. He agreed and said it would be ready in four days. But it wasn't fixed when I returned nor was it ready the next time I visited. It took me one whole month going back and forth from that dealership, but the man kept telling me to come tomorrow after tomorrow.

So I got tired of this and asked him to give me back my money or to let me buy another car. He refused, saying I'd bought the car and could repair it myself or go to hell. He ordered me to leave his property or he was going to call the police, but I refused to leave and told him to call the police. He did so and I thought they would straighten things out. The dealer lied to the police that he had assured me the car would be ready the next day. The police told me to return the next day and didn't ask about my side of the story.

Abraham and I then left his property and then went back on the following day, but we found that the car was not fixed. I then asked him one more time to give me back my money and we argued. He then started to grasp me and to push me out of the place, but I refused to leave. He told me that he could kill me like a dog and nothing would happen to him because this was his country and I was a foreigner. I told him that human life is precious everywhere in the world and I therefore believed that the government of the United States would care about me, even if I were not an American citizen.

He then called the police again. The police said I should leave and not come back or they could take me to jail. I then left the property and asked Abraham what I should do next. He advised me to take the case to the court. Some of my friends who were terrified by the incident told me to inform the news people and then one of my friends told me to go to the DMV and report the case to them.

I followed the last suggestion. One of the DMV officers was appointed to deal with my case and he said he was going to call me back after he had investigated what was going on. In a month, he called and told me that the car was fixed and had passed the inspection. The officer then asked me to go back to the dealership and take my car, but I told him that I was not going to go back there without a law enforcement officer. He agreed to go to the dealer with me the next day. After two months of struggle, I finally had my transportation.

    I continued working and going to school. After about six months, I completed the high school requirements. That lifted a lot of the weight I was carrying and at last I had some time to call my friends and socialize with then.

Chapter 32: Finding Love

One day, I called my cousin Garang Jel who was living in Mississippi and asked him whether he knew where one of the lost girls called Nancy Abur was living. He told me that she used to live there, but had recently moved to North Carolina where her younger sister and brother were attending high school. I told him that Nancy and I used to like each other when we were in Africa and I was interested in talking with her.

Garang called Nancy and then connected me with her on the phone. Nancy and I talked and exchanged numbers. Soon we were talking every day and became boyfriend and girlfriend. After a couple of months, I invited Nancy to visit me in Las Vegas. We spent some days together and we then got engaged before she went home. A couple of months later, I visited her. While I was in North Carolina, we came to the agreement that I should move there since Nancy was staying with her siblings. That would give us time to get to know one another before we got married. I did not wish to move away from Las Vegas because it is a very beautiful city to live in, but I agreed because Nancy was the only parent to her siblings, as they too had lost their mother and father.

I moved to High Point, N.C. in September 2005 and started to apply for jobs. I got hired for a second shift position as a material handler at Furniture Land South, one of the world's largest furniture companies. I went back to school in 2006 at the Guilford Technical Community College in Jamestown and begin to take classes in engineering as a pre-major.

Nancy and I stayed close to one another for several months and we decided in April 2006 to get married on September 2nd. Nancy and I then informed our relatives and friends about our wedding plans and everyone was happy. We began to send out invitation cards early to more than three hundred people.

As Nancy and I were waiting for our day of happiness, something terrible happened. On June thirtieth, Peter Akot, Karlos Akuer, Cornelius Achuil and I decided to visit our friends who were living in Atlanta. We left High Point around 6:00 p.m. We traveled for about four hours and when we had reached the border between South Carolina and Georgia, we lost control of the car because one of the drivers in the other lane was about to hit our car. We came out of the lane into the opposite traffic lane where a big truck hit our car, killing Cornelius on the spot. Karlos was severely injured, including a brain injury and was in a coma. Peter and I were injured, but not as badly. He suffered broken ribs and I had a broken bone in my back.

An emergency helicopter took us to a hospital. Two days later, our fellow Sudanese who were living with us in North Carolina came and took Peter and me home, while Karlos remained in an intensive care unit in Atlanta. Cornelius's body was brought back for burial. Soon after, Karlos was brought back and admitted at the Moses Cone Hospital where he spent several months.

Despite my pain, Nancy and I got married as planned with more than 300 people in attendance. Our wedding day was one of the most beautiful and best days of my life despite the sorrow over Cornelius's death. I wished that I could have enjoyed my wedding with him. I always pray to God to pardon all Cornelius's sins, bless his soul and keep him in his right hand in heaven forever and ever until the day I meet him again.

Nancy and I now are living together as one body, husband and wife who suffered and have almost the same story. From unaccompanied children who were chased out of their homeland by civil war, Nancy and I are now the parents of a daughter, Amelia Aker. Both of us now are attending college. I am working on my bachelor's degree in public health and Nancy is working on her bachelor's in business and computer technology. In addition, we became United States citizens in late 2010. My brother Acien is attending college in Atlanta. He is majoring in business administration and management; he became a citizen in 2008.

As I prepare in mid 2011 to share my life story with all who will listen, one of those responsible for the twists and turns I've experienced, Osama Bin Laden, is no more. Still, I relate my life's journey with the hope that one day others will not experience the hard life I have gone through because of politicians using religion as a tool of terrorism and the destruction of innocent lives. I hope and pray that separating politics and religion will help to make the world a peaceful place instead of a slaughterhouse.

As always, I believe with God's help, that destination is within our reach.

CPSIA information can be obtained at www.ICGtesting.com
Printed in the USA
BVOW011106061011

272924BV00002B/1/P